Essential Siem Reap

The essential guide to Siem Reap and temples of
Angkor.
By Rodney L'Huillier

Table of Contents

Hello Siem Reap

Siem Reap is home to the ancient temples of Angkor, the wonderous UNESCO protected ruins of a civilization whose beginnings date back to 1000BC. To come to Siem Reap is much more than a holiday, it's a connection to an ancient culture, not only in its archaeology but also the living culture within its people.

Modern Siem Reap offers something for everyone, the solo traveler, the couple, the family and the large Asian tour groups can all find a safe and welcoming place here. Whether you want to party all night, and hit the adventure trails all day, or simply take in the temples and relax the afternoons away, it's all possible.

The city is also becoming very multi-lingual, with English being widely spoken, along with it not being too difficult to find speakers of French, Chinese, Japanese, Korean, Thai and many other languages. It's also a city catering to the many different cultures of its visitors with it being easy to find Chinese, Korean, Indian, Japanese, Halal and Western restaurants.

Whilst catering to a multi-cultural audience, the local daily life for locals is very proudly Khmer, a society that smiles through adversity holds onto Buddhism as it's core belief, and is proud of its ancient heritage. Khmer culture is deep and fascinating, although it is somewhat buried beneath the tourist nature of the city and business opportunity which it presents if you are open to it, it will surely find you.

In this guide, I am going to highlight the essential highlights of the city, places to see, things to do, what to eat and where and so much more. It's intended that this book would be used in conjunction with an internet connection and access to the online map at https://goo.gl/5eibLQ and see https://goo.gl/WckTA2 for a live links page and any book updates.

Fast Facts

Cambodia

Country: The Kingdom of Cambodia (Khmer: Kampuchea)

Language: Khmer with English, and some French, widespread in major cities

Capital: Phnom Penh

Dialing code: +855

Time: GMT +7

Currency: Cambodian Riel although the US dollar is the predominant currency used in daily life ($1 = 4000 Riel)

Population: 15.76 million (2016)

Bordering Countries: Vietnam, Thailand, and Laos

Major Airports: Siem Reap, Phnom Penh, and Sihanoukville

Official religion: Theravada Buddhism

GDP: 64 Billion USD (PPP) - 20 Billion USD (Nominal)

Minimum Wage: 153 USD per Month

Siem Reap

Siem Reap Province population: 896,309

Siem Reap city population: 230,714

Districts: 12

Communes: 100

Villages: 907

Peak visitor months: November to March

4

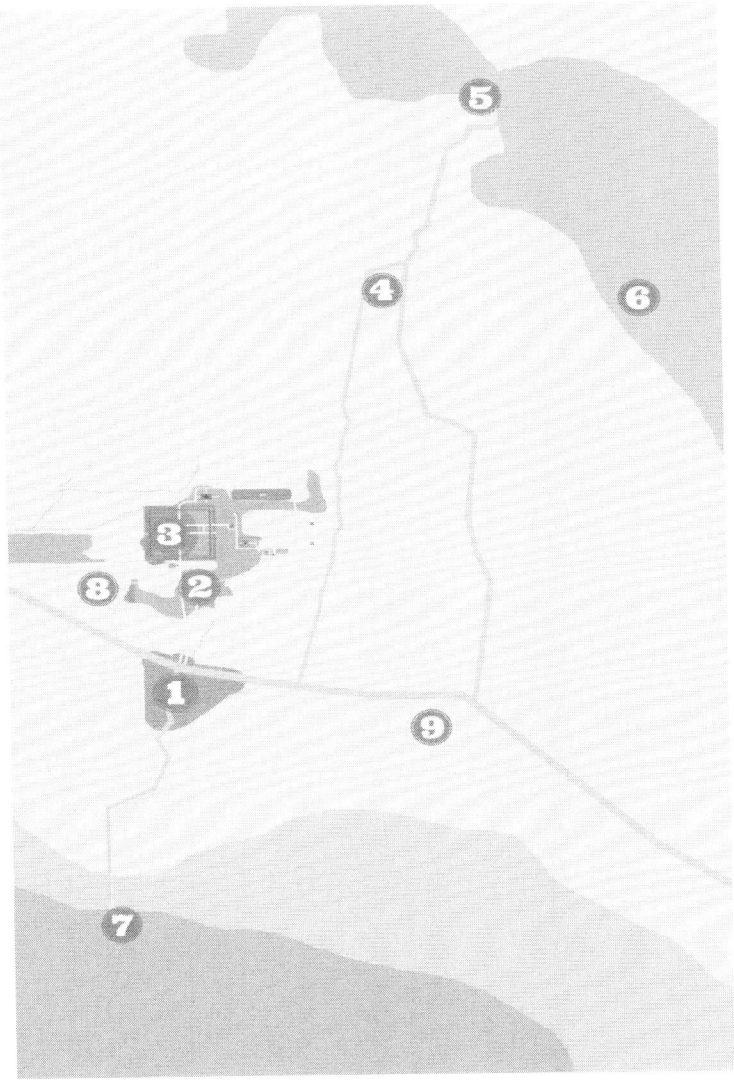

Map: 1. Siem Reap city centre 2. Angkor Wat 3. Angkor Thom 4. Banteay Srey 5. Kbal Spean 6. Phnom Kulen 7. Tonle Sap 8. Airport 9. Rolous Group Temples - See an online map at https://goo.gl/5eibLQ

Angkor visitor numbers by month

Angkor Archaeological Park Visitor numbers by month (2016/2017)

August 172,046

September 130,856

October 165,548

November 219,052

December 249,482

January 287,041

February 251,754

March 225,351

April 181,220

May 147,011

June 140,760

July 182,632

Arriving in Siem Reap

By Bus

Buses arrive from Thailand and Vietnam and terminate at either the Chong Kov Sou Bus Station or at the office of the bus company. The Chong Kov Sou Bus Station is about a $3-4 tuk-tuk ride from the Old Market/Pub Street area, and you need not worry, there will always be plenty of tuk-tuks available.

Arriving by Boat

Not that common any more but it is an option. If you are traveling from Battambang or Phnom Penh you can take a boat which terminates at the Chong Kneas Ferry Dock which is about 15 km from the Old Market/Pub Street area and about $5-7 in a tuk-tuk. Again, there are sure to be no shortage of tuk-tuks available.

Arriving by Air

You'll be flying into Siem Reap Airport which is located about 13km from the Old Market/Pub Street area and about $6 and up in a tuk-tuk. See more in the Siem Reap Airport and Flights section.

Visas

There are two types of visa available on arrival

Tourist Visa (T type) - which lasts for 30 days and allows for single entry, meaning if you leave Cambodia you will need to get another visa on your return. This visa can be extended for another thirty days which can be done via numerous travel agents in Siem Reap.

Ordinary Visa (E type) - is also valid for 30 days and allows for single entry, meaning if you leave Cambodia you will need to get another visa on your return. This visa type can be extended for 1 month or 3 months. This type of visa can also be extended for 6 and 12 months with multiple entries available, meaning you don't need to get a new visa every time you leave Cambodia and return. For 6 and 12-month extensions, you will require a letter of employment from a local business. Again, extensions can be done via local travel agents.

Suggested Travel Agents for Visa extensions

W.E.T Travel - http://worldexpresstour.com - High School Rd, Wat Damnak, Siem Reap

Sopheak Na Travel and Tours - http://sopheaknatravel.com - Tep Vong Road, Sangkat Svay Dangkum, Siem Reap

Online E-Visa - You can also apply for a visa in advance, called an e-visa, not to be confused with the e-type ordinary visa, is equivalent to a Tourist Visa. You can make the application online and the cost is the same bar an additional $6 USD processing fee. Visit: https://www.evisa.gov.kh

Things to do and see

I'm sure your main focus is going to be temple exploring but It's not unusual to get temple overload, so be sure to mix things up with a few alternate attractions.

Get an Aerial View of Angkor and Siem Reap

Angkor Ballooning - http://www.angkorballooning.com - offering two flights per day at sunrise and sunset depending on conditions. Located on airport road. Cost $15 for adults and $7.50 for children.

Microlight Cambodia - http://microlightcambodia.net - offering a range of 20 min, 30 minute and 1-hour packages that give you an unmatched aerial view over the temples, the lush jungle surrounds and even out to the floating villages of Tonle Sap.

Helicopters Cambodia - http://helicopterscambodia.com - offering a range of packages beginning with 8 minute Angkor Wat flight, 14 minute Angkor and nearby temples, 20 minute Angkor Wat and Floating village, the 30 minute Angkor Wat plus Rolous Group Temples plus Floating Village. Prices begin at $95.

Take a cooking class

Take more home than just souvenirs, take home a new skill. Suggested places are

Le Tigre de Papier - https://www.letigredepapier.com - Duration 3h. Classes begin at 10:00, 13:00 and 17:00 Includes market visit and learning one starter, main and dessert. $15 - Pub Street.

Sojourn Boutique Villas - http://sojournsiemreap.com - Duration 3h. Classes begin at 9:30 and 12:30 and includes learning about local customs and beliefs, and hands-on cooking. $24 - Treak Village Rd, Treak Village

Siem Reap Countryside Cooking Class - http://countrysidecookingclass.com - 4h. Classes begin at 8:00 and 14:00 and include local market tour and fabulous countryside setting. A not for profit with a percentage of proceeds supporting the local community. Taphul Road.

Take a yoga class

Peace Cafe - http://peacecafeangkor.org - offers yoga classes, meditation, monk chats, and vegetarian cooking classes.

Angkor Bodhi Tree - http://angkorbodhitree.com - retreat and meditation/yoga classes

Angkor Zen Garden - http://angkorzen.com - meditation and yoga retreat.

Watch an Apsara Dance Performance

Apsara Terrace - http://raffles.com/siem-reap/ - at the Raffles Grand Hotel D'Angkor is known for its impressive classical dance and martial arts performances - $46 inc Buffet - 19:00 to 21:00 - Raffles Grand Hotel D'Angkor, 1 Vithei Charles De Gaulle, Khum Svay Dang Kum

Angkor Village Apsara Theatre - https://www.angkorvillageresort.asia/apsara-theatre/ - Beautiful, elegant setting limited to 40 or so people. Apsara dance show and set menu $25. - 19.30 to 21.30 - Wat Bo Rd

Kulen II Restaurant - http://www.koulenrestaurant.com - Apsara dance show and buffet offering western and Khmer cuisine $12 - Buffet starts at 6 pm and show begins at 7.30pm. - Sivatha Blvd.

See the section on Apsara Dance section for more.

Discover Cambodian Culture through performance

Bambu Stage Siem Reap - http://bambustage.com - 3 different shows on offer, Mon, Wed, Thu & Sat it's Bambu Puppets, on Tuesday there is the 'Temples Decoded' show and banquet $25, and Friday it's the 150 Years of Photography in Photos - Tangram Garden Restaurant, Wat Damnak Village, Sala Komroeuk Commune

Watch the Acclaimed Phare Circus Performance

Phare The Cambodian Circus - https://pharecircus.org - Uniquely Cambodian stories told through performing arts. Nightly beginning at 8 pm, with a series of shows on rotation - $18 with discounts for children - Sok San Rd

Visit Honeybees

Bees Unlimited - http://www.beesunlimited.com - head one hour out of town into scenic rural Cambodian and experience one of the few remaining places that practice traditional Rafter Beekeeping. Transport is included. They also offer a range of other tour options.

Visit the Butterflies

Banteay Srey Butterfly Centre - http://angkorbutterfly.com - features a free-flying garden containing thousands of native species of butterflies - 09.00 to 16.30 - $4 adults $2 Children - Road 67 (on the way to Banteay Srey)

Learn Khmer Martial Arts

Perhaps not as well known as other forms of martial arts but they are having something of a renaissance. The three most popular forms are Pradal Serey which is a form of kickboxing which some believe is the predecessor of Muay Thai, Bokator which is a form of close-quartered combat using styles mimicking animals, and Bok Cham Bab a type of wrestling. Check out http://angkorfightclub.com and http://mrlygym.com

Visit a Museum

Angkor National Museum - http://angkornationalmuseum.com - 8 separate galleries presenting Angkorian history, culture, beliefs and ancient artifacts - 08.30 to 18.30 - No.968 Vithei Charles de Gaulle Road.

Preah Norodom Sihanouk-Angkor Museum - http://apsaraauthority.gov.kh - contains a range of exhibits and items extracted from the temples of Angkor Archaeological Park in particular Banteay Kdei temple. Closed on Mondays. - 08.00 to

17.00 - Entry $3 - Apsara Road just past the Angkor Archaeological Park Ticket Centre.

Angkor Panorama Museum - http://www.angkorpanoramamuseum.com - Located beside the Angkor ticket office and sharing the same car park, the new museum was a donation from the North Koreans. It contains large wall maps and a large model of the Angkor Archaeological Park which is helpful for getting your bearings. The main feature is the 360 panoramic painting depicting the fall and rise of the Khmer Empire in the Jayavarman VII period. Free to enter and $15 to enter the panorama section. - 08.00 -17.00 - Apsara Road

Asian Traditional Museum - http://www.mgcattmuseum.com - showcases traditional textiles of Cambodia, India, Laos, Myanmar, Thailand and Vietnam - Closed on Tuesdays - Entry $3 - 08.30 to 16.00 - Apsara Road opposite Angkor ticket office.

The Cambodian Landmine Museum and Relief Facility - http://cambodialandminemuseum.org - the collection of defused landmines and exhibits - 07.30 to 17.30 - Entry $5 - Road 67, Banteay Srei.

Siem Reap War Museum - http://warmuseumcambodia.com - an insight into Cambodia's war years - 8:00 to 17:30 - Entry $5 - off Hwy 6, behind Royal Angkor International Hospital.

Visit a Pagoda

The key pagodas in the central area are Wat Damnak Pagoda, Wat Bo Pagoda, Wat Thmei Pagoda, Wat Kesararam and Wat Athvea Pagoda. See the section dedicated to Pagodas.

Engage with Local Craftsmen

Artisans d'Angkor - http://artisansdangkor.com - you can witness traditional ceramic, silver and wood crafts made before your eyes. They also have a large store - 07.30 to 17.30 ' Steung Thmei St.

Pouk Silk Farm - http://artisansdangkor.com - learn about local silk production and textiles - 08.00 to 17.30 ' Located in Pouk district, 20 minutes from Siem Reap. Free buses available at 9.30 am and 1.30 pm from the Artisans d'Angkor site on Steung Thmei St.

Khmer Ceramics Centre - http://khmerceramics.com - Traditional Khmer pottery and ceramics made on-site, available for purchase but more excitingly, you can try your hand at making your own - 08.00 to 20.00 - Charles De Gaulle Road.

Sombai - http://www.sombai.com - learn how local rice wine is made and experience the multitude of flavored wines. Workshop tour packages available or visit at will for tasting and purchase.

Go Swimming

Most hotels and even many hostels have pools, and most are open to the public with a fee and some for free. See the Swimming Pools and Gyms section.

Play Golf

Angkor Golf Resort - https://www.angkor-golf.com - Designed by Nick Faldo the world-class course features 18 holes and modern facilities. Club hire is also available - 06.00 to 17.30 - Prices start at $103 - Kasekam Village, Sra Nga

Angkor Wat Putt Putt - http://www.angkorwatputt.com - 14 hole Miniature Golf Course around 9 accurate replicas of the Angkor Temples - 07:30 to 22:00 - $5 and up - out past Sala Kamreuk Rd, see website for directions.

Visit the Cultural Village

The Cambodian Cultural Village - http://www.cambodianculturalvillage.com/en - designed with the intention to give visitors an insight into local culture and traditions featuring 13 unique replica villages, which represent difference cultural heritages with 8 different show performances - 08.00 to 19.00 - Entry $9 and free for children under 1.1m - Hwy 6

Watch a Movie

Platinum Cinema - http://platinumcineplex.com.kh/siem-reap/ - a modern cinema offering 3D movies in air-conditioned comfort.

Angkor Cinema - http://angkorcinema.com - private cinema

located in the Angkor Trade Centre

Get a Massage

Siem Reap has a massage shop on almost every corner and you won't need to walk far in the tourist areas without hearing "massage, sir". Several places offer foot massages beginning at $3 per half hour and up from there. Of course, you can get all types of body massages and that even extends to beauty services. Fish foot massages are also everywhere for no more than a few dollars. Enjoy as you please.

For a more serene spa-style experience you may want to keep walking and try one of these:

Marrison Spa - http://www.marrisonboutiquespa.com - The new and ultra clean establishment is what you expect a massage experience to be, aromatic, peaceful and serene. They offer hot and cold jacuzzi, wet and dry steam rooms and a wide range of massage and beauty services. Prices start from $5 for sauna use and the basic massage begins at $15. Recommended.

Bodia Spa - http://www.bodia-spa.com - offers a full range of massage, aromatherapy, body treatments and scrubs, facial treatments, and more. Massages begin at $33 for 90 min which is on the high side for the city, but this is also the high end of sensory experiences in the city.

Go Horse Riding

Happy Ranch Horse Farm - https://www.thehappyranch.com - offers countryside trail rides from 1 to 4 hours - Angkor Pets Road off Sok San Road

Take a Tour

In the central area of the city travel agents and tour booking agencies can be found every couple of hundred meters, most simply charge a small fee, eg, $1 on top off a $7 fare or may take a commission from the tour provider. Alternatively, you can book buses, tours and so on directly with the provider. Some highlights are listed below.

Angkor Zipline - https://angkorzipline.com - Located in the Angkor Archaeological Park you can fly like a bird on the zipline course featuring 21 platforms and 3 sky-bridges. The company also offers combo tours with Zipline + Quadbike or Zipline + cooking class and many others including transfers.

Quad Adventure Tours - http://www.quad-adventure-cambodia.com - Explore the countryside, villages, and temples by quad bike. Offering half-day, full-day, and overnight tours suitable for all rider skill levels.

Bicycle tours with Grasshopper Adventures - https://www.grasshopperadventures.com - Operating across Asia, Grasshopper Adventures offer a multitude of half-day, full-day, and multi-day tours on bicycles in Siem Reap and throughout Cambodia.

Siem Reap Food Tours - https://www.siemreapfoodtours.com - Learn about Cambodian culture and life through its cuisine on a personal guided tour of the local dishes, markets and more.

Ayana Journeys - http://ayanajourneys.com - Take in Cambodia from a spiritual perspective with a choice of half day and multi-day tour options. Packages offer an introduction into Cambodian folklore and culture whilst other packages offer multi-day educational journeys into Buddhism, local beliefs, and culture.

Siem Reap Shuttle - https://www.siemreapshuttle.com - Via a fleet of vehicles they offer several tour packages including Angkor Temples, Phnom Kulen Waterfall, Kampong Phluk, Banteay Srey, Koh Ker and Beng Melea.

Tara Boat Tour - http://www.taraboat.com - A sunset dinner cruise of Tonle Sap that begins in the afternoon and includes a lotus farm, floating villages, crocodile and fish farm, plus free buffet dinner and all you can drink for $36 including transfers. The company also offers a number of other half day and full day tour choices.

Wildlife and Nature Tours - https://samveasna.org - The Sam Veasna Center offers a wide range of tours which covers the areas of Keo Seima, Tonle Sap, The Northern Plains, The Eastern Plains to include rare birdlife, primates and much more.

Siem Reap Countryside Life Tour with Vespa Adventures - http://vespaadventures.com/siem-reap-bike-tours/ - The group tour, riding Vespas, takes you off the beaten path for a deeper insight into local life inc. visiting a local market, Sugar Palm juice harvester, a Buddhist pagoda, Khmer fortune telling, a temple under restoration, picnic lunch, and much more. Tour goes from 8:00 ' 15.00

Visit Banteay Srei district - http://www.visitbanteaysrei.com - much more than just the location of one of the most beautiful temples, it's a destination offering a real connection with local life and nature. Tours offered include homestays with discovery visits to local farms to learn the art of rice cropping, cooking and local ingredient classes, wildlife excursions, experience village life, visiting local schools and even volunteering.

Angkor Archaeological Park

The term Angkor represents much more than just Angkor Wat or a group of temples, it encompasses an ancient civilization and culture belonging to the ancestors of all Cambodians, something which lives in their hearts, and forms their national identity.

You are visiting more than ancient temples and walking through a historic UNESCO site, you are walking into the heart of the people and into their very soul. I am sure, when you first lay your eyes upon Angkor you are going to have this very feeling.

For many Cambodians, that I have been so fortunate to get to know, they reflect on the time of their ancestors with a very special kind of warmth. A time when they lived from the heart, not fabricating items for money, or toiling for gain, they were driven by joy and love and to create for their community, their culture, and their king.

The park itself covers some 400 square kilometers, a geographical region with hundreds of temples, monuments, and infrastructure that dates back to the 9th century. It was home to the Khmer Empire which flourished from it's beginning until the 15th century and created what is now known as being the largest pre-industrial city in the world. Scientists now believe the city was over 1000 sqm in size and perhaps supporting a population of over one million. The recent airborne lidar scanning of the region completed by Australian archaeologist Dr Damien Evans is still being disseminated for insights into this ancient society, more here https://goo.gl/UXTH86.

I couldn't help wondering, what it would have been like in its heyday? I surely must have been a sight beyond belief, gleaming in white and gold, the lush green surrounds and blue waters. Check out this Digital Reconstruction of Angkor Wat from the Smithsonian Institute https://goo.gl/tstJjZ

Apsara Authority

The temples of Siem Reap are spread out over a massive area which all comes under the banner of Angkor Archaeological Park which in turn is managed by the Apsara Authority http://apsaraauthority.gov.kh with their visitor information site being http://www.angkor.com.kh.

In 2016 a total of 2,197,254 tickets generating some 62,582,200 USD over which the authority has financial autonomy using funds for preservation, development of tourism, sustainable development for poverty reduction and management of the site. The figures and where the funds go is, as it would be in any country, a hotly debated political issue. I will leave it that.

The busiest months for ticket sales are November through to March with the busiest month being December and the slowest month being June.

Visiting the temples

You can buy a one-day ($37), three-day ($62), or seven-day ticket ($72).

The three day and seven-day tickets do not have to be used consecutively as the three-day ticket is valid for 10 days and the seven-day ticket is valid for one month.

Tickets can only be purchased from the Angkor Archaeological Park Ticket Centre at the corner of Road 60 and Aspara Road. The ticket centre opens at 5.00 AM and closes at 5.30 PM. You can now pay for tickets with credit card (Visa, Mastercard, UnionPay, JCB, Discover and Diners Club) and in USD. There is also an ABA ATM onsite and also a few stalls selling snacks, drinks, hats and touristy stuff.

While the centre opens at 5.00 AM in time for sunrise viewing it's not quite early enough to buy a ticket and secure a good position. Fortunately, You can also buy your tickets after 4.30pm and have free entry on that night and access all the next day. So, you can catch a sunset that night, and then of course back the next day for a full day of temple exploring. I suggest getting to the ticket office at 4 pm so you can get up the front of the line and get away as early as possible to find a great sunset watching spot.

Temple visiting times

All the temples are open from 7:30 am to 5:30 pm, except for:

- Angkor Wat and Srah Srang are open from 5:00 am to 5:30 pm
- Phnom Bakheng and Pre Rup, from 5:00 am to 7:00 pm
- Banteay Srei closes every day at 5:00 pm
- Kbal Spean closes at 3:00 pm

Visitor Code of Conduct

It's worthy to remember that Angkor is a very sacred site, not only in the hearts of Khmer but also for many Hindu and Buddhist who make pilgrimages here.

As a basic guide:

Dress respectfully - No shirts and skirts above the knee, no bare shoulders.

Show care - no sitting, leaning, or placing objects on the temple structures.

You can read a full guide here:
http://www.angkor.com.kh/code-conduct

Transport to and around the temples

You have a number of choices being tuk-tuk, private car, bike, scooter and electric scooter.

The most popular means is to hire a tuk-tuk and for a full day expect to pay around $15-25 depending on what you negotiate and what you'd like to see.

A private car will cost a little more at around $35 for a full day in an air-conditioned mini-van or SUV inc. driver and fuel.

In both of the above cases, you can negotiate your plans with the driver depending on whether you are doing one day or multi days, and most drivers are very knowledgeable and will help you plan the best itinerary according to your schedule.

If you like to go your own way, you are welcome to do so, hire a scooter for between $8-15 (see the transport section) and chart your own course. You can also hire an electric scooter from Green e-bike which has recharging stations throughout the park.

You can also hire a bike and ride, but do be mindful, this is taxing. Just walking around the temples themselves in the heat of the days here can exhaust most people. But, regardless, many people do it, just plan appropriately.

Which way is best? Up to you, each has their benefits, I enjoyed going in a tuk-tuk and having the local experience of the driver as a guide plus it's very carefree. And I also really enjoyed going my own way on a scooter. Up to you.

Also see the transport section for more details.

Official Temple Guides

Whilst drivers can give you a lot of insight into local culture, and navigate you around the temples, they cannot actually go into the temples with you and be your guide. For that, you need to hire a licensed guide. Only guides licensed by the Ministry of Tourism can guide people through the temple. They must study history and knowledge of the temples before passing an exam to receive their license. They are easy to spot as they all wear khaki colored shirts with an official logo sewn on. These guides can be arranged through tour agencies which are numerous.

The official temple guides can provide you with deep insight into history, the significance of certain places, the culture and the best spots to see.

The Temples

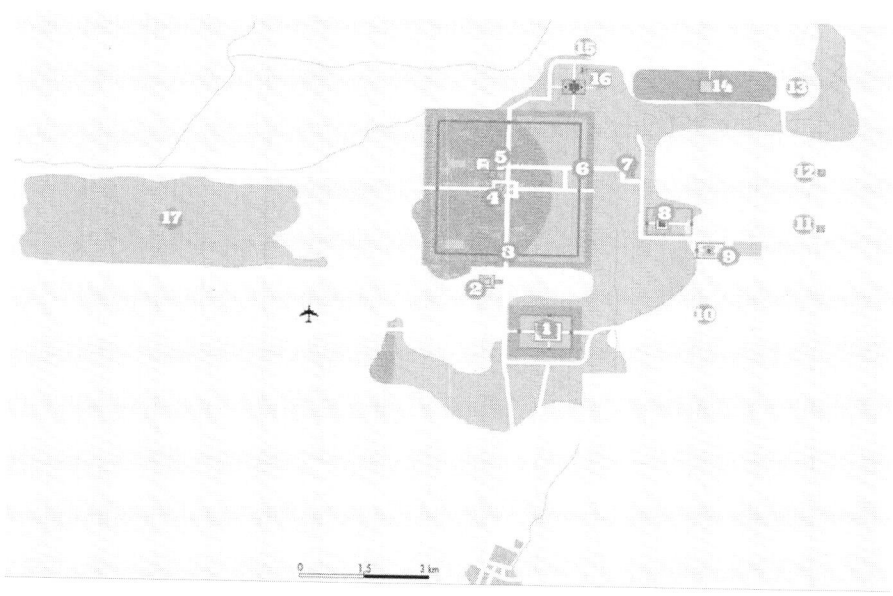

1.Angkor Wat 2 Phnom Bakheng 3. Angkor Thom South Gate 4. Angkor Thom 5 Terrace of the Elephants/Phimeanakas 6. Victory Gate 7. Ta Keo 8. Ta Prohm 9. Banteay Kdei and Srah Srang 10. Prasat Kravan 11. Pre Rup 12. East Mebon 13. Ta Som 14. Neak Pean 15. Prasat Prei/Banteay Prei 16. Preak Khan 17. West Baray Note:1-10 = Small Circuit 11-16 Grand Circuit Online Map: https://goo.gl/5eibLQ

The Temples

Angkor Wat - it's the icon of the nation, the logo on the national flag and the most visited attraction in all of the Angkor Park. You can look at all the pictures you like, it is only when you see it with your own eyes that you grasp the scale, the immensity, the wonder, and are overcome with the feeling of awe.

Those feelings are compounded when your foot takes its first step on the sandstone causeway that takes you across the moat and to the Terrace of Honor, you will be entering the vision of the Khmer King Suryavarman II.

The highlights here include the gallery walls and their bas-reliefs depicting Hindu epics and one with King Suryavarman II himself. Throughout the temple, there are depictions of Apsara and Hindu Deity, more than 1700, all remarkably diverse.

Don't miss the 5-meter statue of the Hindu god Vishnu who apparently had his head replaced with that of the Buddha.

Originally a Hindu temple dedicated to Lord Vishnu it was later converted to a Buddhist temple as it remains so today.

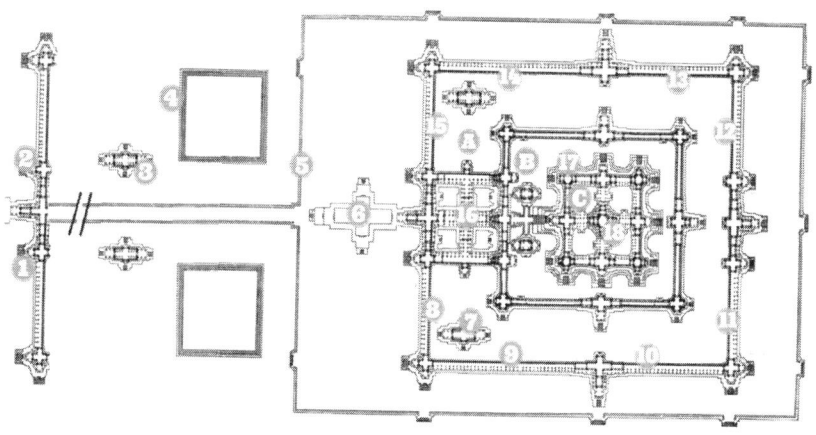

Angkor Wat - 1.Vishnu statue at entry gate 2. Dvarapala statue at entry gate 3. North Library (mirrored by the South Library) 4. Northern Reflection Pond. This marks roughly where to stand for the perfect sunrise shot. (mirrored by the Southern Reflection Pond) 5. Balustrade which surrounds the perimeter. 6. Terrace of Honor 7. South Thousand God Library (mirrored by the North Thousand God Library) 8. Gallery Bas Relief: The Battle of Kurukshetra 9. Gallery Bas Relief: The Historic Parade 10. Gallery Bas Relief: Heaven and Hell 11. Gallery Bas Relief: The Churning of the Ocean of Milk 12. Gallery Bas Relief: The Victory of Krishna over the Asuras 13. Gallery Bas Relief: The Victory of Krishna over the Asura Bana 14. Gallery Bas Relief: The Battle between the Ausuras and the Devas 15. Gallery Bas Relief: The Battle of Lanka 16. 4 sacred ponds and gallery 17. Outer Towers (at each corner) 18. Central Tower. A. First Level - featuring gallery walls depicting scenes from Hindu mythology B. Second level - featuring gallery walls featuring carvings of over 1500 Apsaras, all unique C. Third level - featuring the five towers, representing Mount Meru of Hindu mythology. Once a place only visited by kings and high priests.

24

Angkor Thom - more than a temple, it's a city. Angkor Thom became the new capital center under the reign of King Jayavarman VII and remained so until the end of the empire. It is a walled city surrounded by a moat with five gates containing the temples of Bayon, Preah Palilay, Phimeanakas, Baphuon and Terrace of the Elephants and Terrace of the Leper King. There are 5 gates, each with their own charm. The South Gate, and to a lesser extent Victory Gate and North Gate, are especially impressive with the massive smiling faces and bridges that are lined with gods on the left and demons on the right symbolizing the Hindu myth of the Churning of the Milk-Ocean and the constant battle between good and evil.

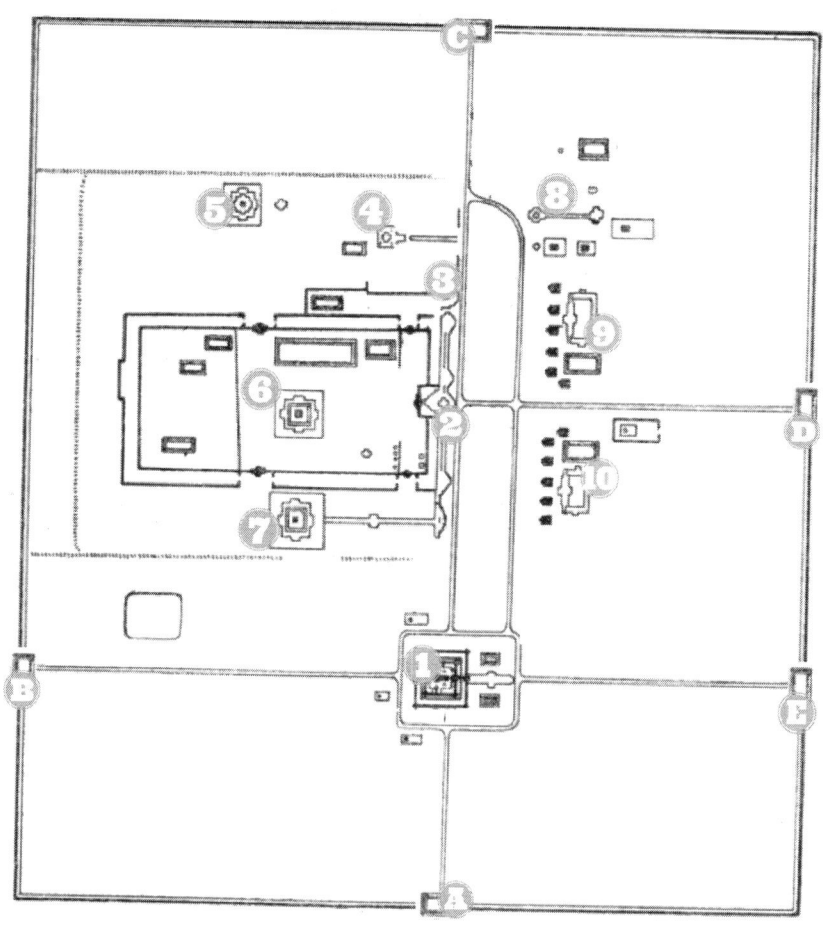

Angkor Thom - 1. Bayon 2. Terrace of Elephants 3. Terrace of the Leper King 4. Tep Pranam 5. Prah Paliliay 6. Royal Palace and Phimeanakas 7. Baphoun 8. Preah Pithu 9. North Kleang 10. South Kleang and Prasat Suor Prat A. South Gate B. West Gate C. North Gate D. Victory Gate E. Gate of the Dead

Bayon Temple - Not to be missed, Bayon is a Buddhist temple featuring 54 four-sided towers with each side depicting the smiling faces of Avalokiteshvara a figure in Buddhist culture representing the perfection of compassion. There are bas-reliefs here depicting Khmer life at that time and the battles they faced. The exact center of the temple was said to represent the intersection of heaven and earth.

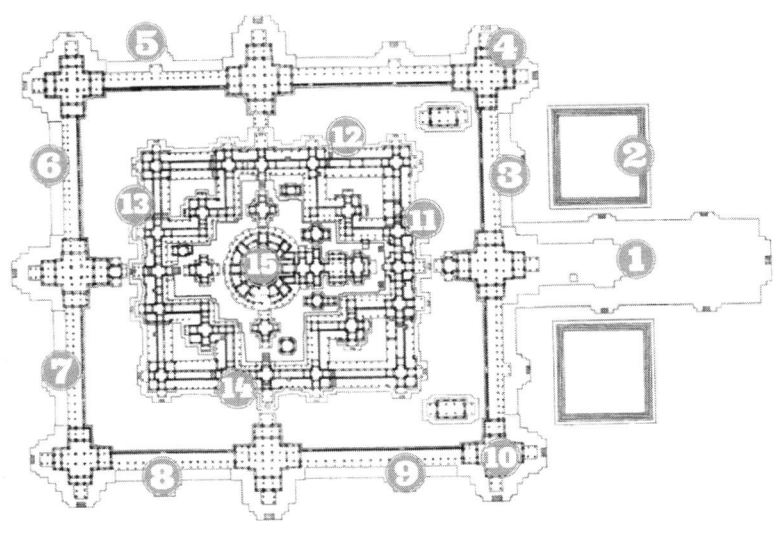

1. Terrace 2. Ponds 3. Bas-Relief: Battle with the Cham 4. Bas-Relief: Procession of the Warriors 5. Bas-Relief: Circus and Animals 6. Bas-Relief: War and Royal Procession 7. Bas-Relief: Military Procession 8 Bas-Relief: Military Procession 9. Bas-Relief: Daily Life with Naval Battle 10. Bas-Relief: Palace 11. Bas-Relief: Story of the Leper King 12. Bas-Relief: Scene from Hindu Mythology 13. Bas-Relief: Scene from Hindu Mythology: Churning of the Ocean of Milk 14. Bas-Relief: Scene from Hindu Mythology featuring Lord Shiva

Baphuon - originally a Hindu temple created to represent Mout Meru from Hindu mythology. It was later converted to Buddhist temple and a reclining Buddha was added but not completed. You can climb to the top and will be rewarded with a superb view of Phnom Bakheng and Phimeanakas.

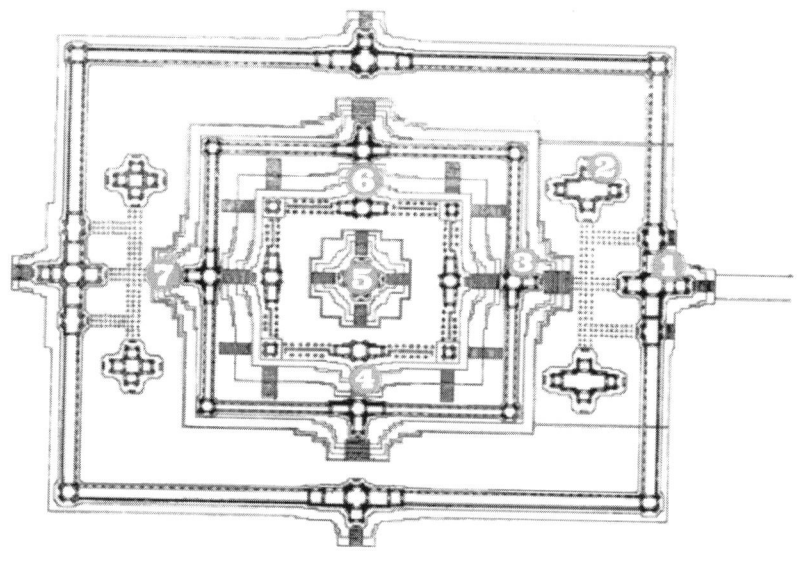

1. Entrance gorupa 2. Library (mirrored on the south) 3. 2 Level galleries - at each of the four entry gorupas you'll find interesting bas-reliefs depicting Hindu mythology and Khmer life 4. Entry stairs to the top level 5. Sanctuary which once held a ligna dedicated to Shiva 6. Exit staircase 7. Western entrance and the part completed reclining Buddha.

Baksei Chamkrong - a 13 m tall stepped pyramid near to Phnom Bakheng.

Banteay Prei - not hugely popular with the tourist crown this small and quite decayed temple does have some interesting carved lintels.

Bat Chum - A small Buddhist temple consisting of a trio of towers.

Banteay Kdei - A Buddhist temple in Bayon style it sits opposite Srah Srang and is similar to Ta Prohm yet far more intact.

Chau Say Tevoda - a small, but neat temple similar in style to the adjacent Thommanon.

Chapel of the Hospital - Near to Ta Keo there is very little left remaining of what would have been a hospital and chapel. Good quiet spot.

East Mebon Temple - an island temple in the middle of the East Baray. While the baray is completely dry the temple remains and features impressive stone carved elephants and impressively detailed carvings depicting figures from Hindu mythology in particular the Hindu god Indra.

Kleangs (North and South) - possible once serving as storage rooms, or perhaps even guest rooms for visiting nobility.

Kravan Temple - built in early times of the Khmer Empire this temple is a little different, firstly that it has been restored and sits on a well kept rubble less site that at certain times of the year is quite grassy. It is also home to some large bas-relief depictions of Vishnu and Lakshmi. Thirdly it uses smaller reddish bricks with an organic mortar.

Krol Ko - a small temple that was perhaps been another hospital chapel. Good quiet spot.

Kutisvara temple - very small temple near to Banteay Kdei, what remains is mostly in ruin.

Neak Pean - or Preah Neak Poan, a small island temple that lies in the middle of the Jayatataka which was the last baray built in the Khmer Empire. There is one centre pool surrounded by four smaller pools which is all believed to once be a ritual bathing site.

Phimeanakas temple - head up the sandstone pyramid from its western side and enjoy an impressive view over the surrounds.

Phnom Bakheng - a hill temple dedicated to Shiva, one of the main deities of Hinduism, and was later converted to a Buddhist temple. The pyramid base has seven levels, representing the seven heavens in Hindu mythology and at the top level, there are five sandstone sanctuaries stand in a quincunx pattern. At the top, you have views over the forest and to Angkor Wat. It's the most popular sunset spot and also the busiest.

Prasat Bei temple - located near the moat of Angkor Thom and Prohm Bakheng, it's a small temple consisting of three towers, which was apparently never completed.

Prasat Prei temple - mostly rubble, this small temple near to Neak Pean does have some carvings remaining.

Prasat Suor Prat - located opposite the southern end of the Terrace of the Elephants these 12 monumental towers are purpose unknown bar locals who suggest they supported a high wire for performances.

Prasat Top (East) - located in Angkor Thom, it is a very small tower built in honor of a famous monk of the time.

Prasat Top (West) - located in Angkor Thom, it's another very small tower, mostly in ruin and believed to be a Buddhist temple.

Preah Khan Temple - a large walled and moated temple featuring processional walkways, towers, ceremonial spaces, courtyards, shrines, reliefs, and a maze of connecting corridors. It's a place less visited than most but it's a must.

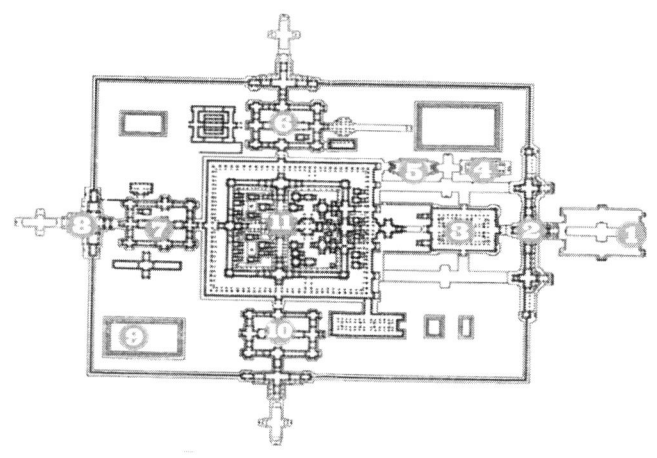

Preah Khan - 1. Stone terrace that is part of a path that connects all the way to Jayatataka Baray 2. East Gorupa 3. Hall of the Dancers (note the impressive lintels) 4. Double story unknown building 5. Library 6. North temple 7. West temple 8. West gorupa 9. Chapel 10. South Temple 11. Central Sanctuary

Preah Palilay - A 33 m long causeway connects it to the single sandstone gopura (a gorupa ornately marks a temples entrance). Before the stone temples there is a shrine with a 3 M tall Buddha statue.

Preah Pithu Group - a cluster of five small temples near to the Terrace of the Elephants. The shady area has a nice ambiance, as for architecture you will find some sculpted lintels and carvings to go hunting for.

Pre Roup Temple - another alternative sunset and sunrise viewing spot, Prae Roup, or Pre Rup, is a three-tiered pyramid base with five lotus towers. It's a recommended spot to visit and has a somewhat impressive stance when viewed from a hundred or so meters back. Take in the views from the top and look for the impressive carvings.

Srah Srang - a man-made lake claimed to be the royal baths, it features a platform opposite Banteay Kdei which is a great spot to watch the sunrise through the trees and over the water. For sunsets head to the opposite eastern end.

Spean Thma - a stone bridge that was at some point constructed from pieces of other nearby temples.

Ta Keo - in its day surrounded by a moat, the large five-storey pyramid base features five towers arranged in that familiar quincunx pattern. Work on the temple was never fully completed yet it remained functioning.

Ta Nei temple - located to the northeast of Angkor Thom's Victory Gate, the beauty of this temple is that it has no car park, and you won't get busloads of tourists. Although, it is not large and mostly in ruin yet it does have some worthy Apsara carvings.

Ta Prohm Temple - one of Angkor's most popular temples, perhaps due do its star role in the Tomb Raider movie and perhaps due to it's unrestored, lost jungle temple feel that makes it so atmospheric and photogenic. Not to be missed is the strangling roots that have woven themselves into the structure, the corridors, and the detailed bas-reliefs.

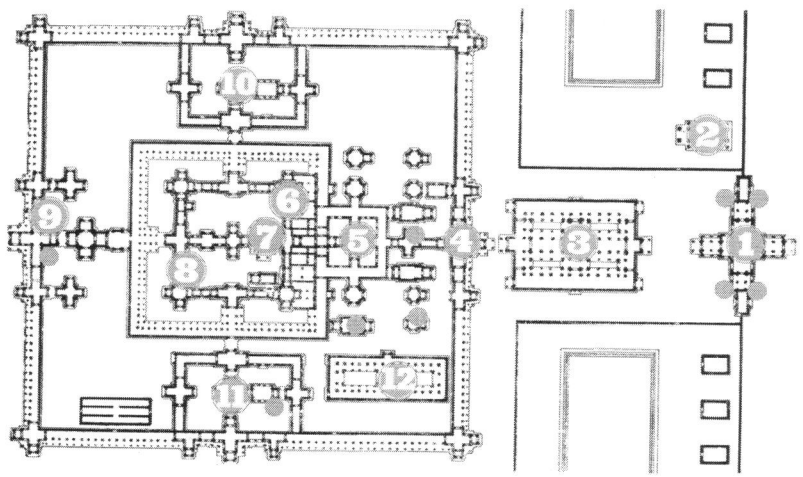

Ta Prohm - 1. East gate gorupa 2. Hall of Fire 3. Hall of Dancers 4. Gorupa to 3rd enclosure 5. Collapsed gallery 6, 8 & 9 Strangler fig trees 7. Central tower9. West gate gorupa 10. North temple 11. South Temple 12. Library. Green Dots: Bas-Reliefs

Ta Prohm Kel - located opposite the northwestern side of Angkor Wat's moat, it's another small hospital chapel. It does have some nice lintels and carvings.

Ta Som - located at the eastern end of Jayatataka (Neak Peans baray) some call this temple a mini Ta Prohm, and it features many detailed carvings, corridors, and galleries.

Tep Pranam - located near Preah Palilay and to the north of the Terrace of Elephants, there is a stone walkway which leads to a large stone Buddha sitting on a lotus flower.

Terrace of the Elephants - forming part of the wall that linked to Phimeanakas, it was a royal viewing deck to watch parades. Notable are the sculpted elephants that feature as part of the wall and from which it draws its name. There are also sculptures of garudas, a mythical bird in Hindu culture, and scenes or dancers and warriors.

Terrace of the Leper King - located at the northern end of the Terrace of Elephants it features deeply carved nagas (deities within Hindu and Buddhist culture), demons and more. It's also home to a seated statue which many claim as being a representation of a former king who was believed to have leprosy, thus why the terrace has its name.

Thma Bay Kaek temple - located outside the South Gate of Angkor Thom, there's not much too look at but it is a really nice shady, grassy spot by the edge of the moat.

Thommanon - a restored temple that is built in the style of Angkor Wat and features some beautiful stone carved lintels and impressive stone carved female devatas.

West Mebon and the West Baray - The West Mebon, the island in the middle of the West Baray doesn't have a lot to offer but that's not to say you won't enjoy a boat ride on the massive lake. The West Baray is perhaps one of the most massive constructions undertaken by the Khmer Empire, dug out by hand this man-made lake is 8km by 2km and had an approximate volume of 43 million cubic meters of water. It's easy to forget that Angkor was a mega-city of the time with near to 1 million people, the water management system was vast and complex with some scientists suggesting a connection between water supply and the fall of the empire.

More? Yes, there is always more, for deeper insight you may enjoy "A Guide to the Angkor Monuments" by Maurice Glaize although written in 1944, from which several images have been drawn and info gleaned, it's still a superb and deep insight into architecture and history. Available freely online: http://goo.gl/Rq583E

Beyond central Angkor

While most of the key historic sites are located centrally and covered by the Small Circuit and Grand Circuit as outlined in the picture above which will probably leave most people with temple overload by the end, there is more. If you want to get off the well-beaten tourist track (to a small degree) take a tuk-tuk/car journey to some of these outer lying attractions.

Banteay Srei - (covered by Angkor pass) - it's perhaps one of the most beautiful temples, restored in 1930's by the French. It it's 3 enclosures it features ponds, libraries, sanctuary, intricate bar-relief carvings, pediments, carved lintels, guardian statues which all make it very worthy of the effort to visit. Banteay Srei is located about 36km from Siem Reap and about 30km from Angkor Wat. It takes about 50 min in a car/tuk-tuk to get there and the journey is just as enjoyable as the destination traveling through rural Cambodia. The trip here can be combined with many other points of interest, see the itinerary ideas further below.

Banteay Samre - (covered by Angkor pass) - is another temple restored by the French. The eastern entrance has a 200m long stone path with balustrade that leads to a terrace guarded by lions and inside you'll find galleries depicting scenes from Hindu mythology along with gorupas and carved lintels. The inner sanctuary also features galleries and central Angkor Wat style tower.

Phnom Krom - (covered by Angkor pass) - a 15-minute journey from Siem Reap city centre and atop a small hill you will find the remains of a Hindu Temple that was built in the 9th century. The Lotus Fields are on the way which has many bamboo hut restaurants serving local foods.

Roluos Group - (covered by Angkor pass) - a 10-minute journey from Siem Reap city centre. The cluster of temples here include Bakong, Lolei, Preah Ko, and Prei Monti. At Bakhong and Lolei there are functioning monasteries, Preah Ko is the oldest temple here and the major attraction os Bakong which was rebuilt by the French in the 1930's. Bakong is also another alternative sunset viewing spot.

Prasat Wat Athvea (Wat Athva) - (covered by Angkor pass) - Near to Chong Kneas at Tonle Sap, the ancient temple is located beside a new functioning Buddhist pagoda. It's only a small temple but it is peaceful and can be visited on the way to Tonle Sap, Phnom Krom or the lotus farms.

Phnom Bok - (covered by Angkor pass) - perhaps one of the oldest temples in the Angkor area. Built by King Yasovarman I in the 9th century it is secluded and not often visited. If you are looking for an untouristed secret temple that's actually worthwhile visiting, then this is probably it. It's a 20km climb to the top, but the views are worthy. Located 25km out of Siem Reap.

Bang Melea - (entry ticket $5 - not included in Angkor pass) - The temple is largely unrestored and it's from natures takeover of the site that it draws most of its charm. It is similar to other temples in that its layout features a moat, three enclosures, and a sanctuary. The site also features several carvings depicting scenes from Hindu mythology. Located about 70km from Siem Reap which will take about one hour by car.

Koh Ker - (entry ticket $10 - not included in Angkor pass) - This is another area which sees few tourists but I am sure that's going to change, visit now and you'll be able to capture it before the herds beat out a path. For a brief time in the early days of the empire it was a capital. Around 96 temples have been discovered so far including Neang Khmao Temple, Pram Temple, Chen Temple, Preng Well, Rampart of Koh Ker Temple, Kuk Temple, Prang Temple, Krahom Temple, Khmao Temple, and Koh Ker Temple. Located around 120 Km from Siem Reap which is about 2.5 hrs by car.

Preah Khan of Kampong Svay - (entry ticket $5 - not included in Angkor pass) - it's a long way out and one of the least explored or restored places. But that may not be for long and if you visit know you'll be one of the ones who visited before it became touristified. It's the largest complex built in the Angkorian period and dates back to the days of Suryavarman I. It features a Bayon style tower with four smiling stone carved faces, Preah Damrei which is a pyramid style temple with two beautiful stone elephants to name a couple of highlights. Located one hour or so from Siem Reap by car.

The Tour Circuits

Choosing what to see and how to navigate it is a headache in waiting, fortunately, early French explorers made this task a little easier leaving us with what they called the small circuit and grand circuit.

The Small Circuit takes in the major temples of Angkor Wat,

Angkor Thom, Ta Phrohm, and Banteay Kdei. It also includes smaller highlights such as Baphoun, The Terrace of the Leper King, Terrace of the Elephants, Prasat Suor Prat, Spean Thma and Srah Srang. It's a full day from at least 8 am to 6 pm!

The Grand Circuit extends the small circuit and includes Preah Khan, Neak Pean to the Eastern Mebon and Ta Som & Pre Roup. The grand circuit would be performed over two whole days at a minimum.

Some examples for half day and full day tours that can be combined for multi-day adventures.

Half Day Angkor Highlights

- South Gate Angkor Thom, Bayon Temple, Terrace of Elephants, Terrace of Leper King, Victory Gate, Ta Prohm & Angkor Wat. Can be done by Tuk-tuk or scooter.

Angkor Small Circuit Full Day

- Angkor Wat, South Gate Angkor Thom, Bayon, Baphuon, Phimeanakas, Terrace of Elephants, Victory Gate, Thommanom, Chau Say Thevoda, Hospital Chapel, Ta Keo, Ta Nei, Ta Prohm, Banteay Kdei & Srah Srang. Can be done by car, tuk-tuk or scooter.

Angkor Grand Circuit Full Day

- Phnom Bakheng, Baksei Chamkrong, Prasat Bei, South Gate Angkor Thom, Terrace of Leper King, Preah Palilay, Tep Pranam, Preah Pithu, North Gate, Banteay Prei, Preah Khan, Neak Pean, Krol Ko, Ta Som, East Mebon, Pre Rup & Prasat Kravan. Can be done by car, tuk-tuk or scooter.

Half Day Rolous Group

- Preah Ko, Bakong, Lolei and Prasat Prei Monti. Can be done by Tuk-tuk or scooter. Can be done by car, tuk-tuk or scooter.

-

Full Day Beng Mealea & Koh Ker

- Beng Mealea is approx 90 mins from Siem Reap and further onto Koh Ker is another 60 minutes drive. Best done by car.

Full Day Banteay Srei

- Banteay Srei, Landmine Museum, Butterfly Garden & Banteay Samre. Best done by car or tuk-tuk.

Banteay Srei & Kbal Spean

- Banteay Srei and then Kbal Spean inside Phnom Kulen National Park. Best done by car.

Common sights on the temple trail

Picture next page 1.Naga 2. Lion 3. Vishnu 4. Devata 5. Apsara 6. Dvarapala 7. Garuda 8. Elephant

Common sights on the temple trail

Apsaras and Devatas - Figures from Hindu mythology, Apsaras, referred to as divine or celestial dancing girls are ubiquitous throughout Angkor featuring in bas-reliefs and on pillars. When depicted in still form as opposed to dancing they are seen as Devata.

Dvarapala - armed with swords or clubs they are protectors of the temples, featuring mostly in bas-reliefs near entrances.

Naga - You'll see this on the end of balustrades and in other artwork. It's a large fan crested multi-headed serpent-like creature who comes from Hindu mythology. Most have seven or nine heads, with an odd number of heads depicting male energy, infinity, timelessness, and immortality, and even number of heads depicting female energy, representing physicality, mortality, temporality, and the earth.

Lion - Lions are guardians, another figure from Hindu mythology.

Elephant - the elephant, white elephants in particular, are seemingly sacred in early Khmer culture, there is one folk story of a king who was mistakenly killed by a farmer and not know who was to succeed they looked to the kings white elephant who went and sat in front of the farmer, thus, the farmer was anointed king.

Vishnu - a powerful god in Hindu mythology, Vishnu was adopted into the local culture of Neak Ta (spirits of nature and ancestors) and known as Ta Reach (the most powerful neak ta in the region).

Gajasimha and Reachisey - a figure from Hindu mythology, being part lion and part elephant. Often seen as temple guardian or being ridden in battle scenes.

Garuda - once again a figure from Hindu mythology, part man part bird and enemy of the naga. The Garuda is often seen in depictions of winning battles.

Lokeshvara - Bodhisattva representing the compassion of the Buddha.

Temple Mountain - the basic underlying scheme for all the temples was that of Temple Mountain, to represent Mount Meru from Hindu mythology.

Quincunx - another representation of Mount Meru with a center tower surrounded by four other temples placed at the corners of a square. Many temples in Angkor take this format such as Pre Rup, Ta Keo and Angkor Wat.

Sanctuary - housing the deity which temple was built to honor.

Prasat - the sanctuary tower.

Goupra - a monument style gateway entrance

Galleries - the walls surrounding the prasats, sometimes enclosed, sometimes open both sides and sometimes open on one side.

Libraries - located at the base near the entrance and built independently of the main temple. Normally opening to the east, at Angkor Wat they open to the east and west.

Naga Bridge - the most popular example is that featured on the bridges of Angkor Thom which uses naga shaped balustrades supported by 54 devas on one side and 54 asuras on the other in a representation of the Hindu story Churning of the Ocean Milk.

Moats - representing the sea, and perhaps having a purpose in relation to maintaining the groundwater table.

False Doors - many prasats have four doors with only the eastern being open and the other three being replicas of the wooden eastern door.

Lintels - intricately stone carved block featuring above doorways and windows, lintels are used extensively.

Colonettes - narrow decorative columns supporting the lintels above.

Pediments - the decorative triangle above the lintel.

Linga - a religious symbolic statue, connected with the Hindu god Shiva, in the shape of a stone post with a smooth curved top.

Bas-reliefs - stone carvings that told stories of Hindu mythology and the life and times of the Khmer Empire. Prominent at Angkor Wat's gallery walls where they are claimed to be the longest set of bas-relief carvings in the world.

Srah and Baray - water reservoirs, examples are the East Baray (now dry), the West Baray, Jayatataka Baray, and the Srah Srang.

Angkor Sunsets and Sunrises

The sunrise at Angkor Wat is perhaps one of the most quintessential experiences, including that photo that overlooks the pond with the reflection of the temple towers and the sun rising above with all that yellowy golden light. It's like a dream! And in most cases, it is, a photoshop created dreamscape. Whilst it is beautiful and very very worthy of the effort to drag yourself out of the hotel bed at 4.30 am, it may not match most of the photos that circulate the internet.

Expectations in check, you have a number of options as to where you choose to go. As a general tip buy your ticket the night before so you don't waste time in the morning at the ticket office, alternatively be at the front door when it opens at 5 AM.

A tip for sunrise watchers, be patient and wait, and wait. The sky will light up and the sun will appear to be a no-show, but don't worry that orange ball of light will come!

Sunrise Spots

Angkor Wat Temple - You need to get here early to get that perfect position, midway along the Northern Reflection Pond and right at the water's edge. Alternatively, some people like to stand back and shoot from the North or South Library.

Ta Prohm Temple - It's not actually a sunrise viewing spot, but a magical sunrise experience as the golden light pours in through the trees.

Phnom Bakheng - There is a 30-minute climb so be sure to factor that in. There are photo opportunities at the foot of the temple capturing the temple itself bathed in the morning light or heading up with the herd, and there will be a herd.

Srah Srang - A rather serene spot to watch the sun rising over the water.

Bayon - a great alternative to the busier spots, the golden light creates quite a surreal experience as lights up the smiling faces of the temple.

Pre Rup - can get a little busy but not as much as Angkor Wat or Bakheng, a short climb up the stairs of the temple and you'll have a great view out over the temple surrounds and forest.

Sunset Spots

Phnom Bakheng Hill - Pretty much as per the sunrise above except you'll be watching a sunset.

Angkor Wat West Side - Go to Angkor Wat's moat on the west side (opposite Ta Prohm Kel) and there's a nice grassy strip in front of the moat.

Angkor Wat East Side - on the side of Ta Kao entrance follow the moat up and find a grassy spot to watch the sun behind, Angkor Wat.

Angkor Wat Ponds - Stand on the eastern side of the northern pond and watch the sunset of the library.

Pre Rup - As per sunrise

Banteay Srei - take a seat at the edge of the inner moat enjoy a perfect time for photos as the sun sets behind the temple.

Banteay Samre - watch the sun set behind it's Angkor Wat style tower from the east side.

Phimeanakas - watch the sun set behind the temple.

Neak Pean - watch the sunset over the water.

Bakong (Rolous Group) - either climb up and watch the sunset over the temple or watch the sunset behind the temple from ground level

Pagodas in Siem Reap

Theravada Buddhism is the official religion in Cambodia and has existed in the country since the 5th century. Today it is practiced by 95 percent of the population and you won't need to go far to find a pagoda or shrine in Siem Reap, or throughout the regional areas.

The pagoda, or Wat, is considered the spiritual center of the village and traditionally each village will have one. This is very much the case in Siem Reap Province. The typical pagoda features a walled complex containing a sanctuary with statues of Buddha, residences for the monks, a large hall, rooms for study and lectures, stupas which contain the remains of family members, and garden areas.

Many of the pagodas are quite beautiful, featuring traditional Khmer architecture, with lots of red and gold along with very colorful sections

Men who join to become monks usually only do so on a temporary basis, and monks do not make perpetual vows, although some will stay on permanently. Most men over 16 will join a temple as it's held in high regard to do so. Of course, there are also nuns yet they are far outnumbered and are mostly subservient to monks.

In the mornings you'll notice pairs of monks wandering around town and dropping by local businesses to give blessings. The monks will perform a brief chant and the business owner will offer a small donation. If you are at the business at the time there is no need for you to make an offering.

Visiting a Pagoda

Remember to dress appropriately, covering from shoulders to knees, take your hat off, and take your shoes off when you enter the pagoda. Always ask permission before photographing monks.

The Pagodas

Wat Damnak - it's the largest in Siem Reap and hosts a primary school and Centre for Khmer Studies. Located at the southern end of Wat Bo Road.

Wat Bo Pagoda - it's the oldest pagoda in Siem Reap being built in the 18th century. Located behind Gloria Jeans on Street 22.

Wat Preah Prom Rath Pagoda - it's one of most beautiful pagodas in the city, and the most central. It features many statues and intricate wall paintings. Located on Pokambor Avenue at the end of street 9.

Wat Thmei Pagoda - the pagoda features a memorial to the people that were killed right in this area during the Khmer Rouge era - located behind Le Meridian Hotel

Wat Kesararam Pagoda - contains some very beautiful murals of the life of Buddha, pristine grounds and memorial to people who died in the area during the Khmer Rouge era. - on NR6 near to Sokkha Resort.

Wat Preah Enkosei - built on the site of an early Angkorian brick Hindu temple (1000 AD) which remains standing - Located on River Road towards the Road 60 end.

Po Banteaychey Pagoda - Containing some wonderful statues and color wall murals, it's worth a visit if you are out that way - off Road 63

Shrine to Preah Ang Chek, Preah Ang Chorm & Ya Tep - hailed as the protectors of Siem Reap and it's people, Preah Ang Chek & Preah Ang Chorm were believed to have originally come from Angkor Wat. In the middle of the road beside these is a temple containing a statue of Ya Tep (Neak Ta) who is a very ancient figure in Cambodian beliefs representing a kind of energy which unites community and nature. Many will visit there wishing for luck. - Located on NR6 adjacent to the Royal Gardens.

The Tonle Sap

Tonle Sap is an icon of the country alongside Angkor Wat and a natural wonder in its own right. For part of the year it becomes largest freshwater lake in Asia as flows from the Mekong River mid-year start to head down the Tonle Sap River causing the lake to grow in size tenfold over the coming months, then, as the level in the Mekong drops, the flow of the Tonle Sap returns to normal and water starts draining from the lake back into the Mekong.

It's a very special eco-habitat providing a home and breeding ground to over 300 species of freshwater fishes, as well as snakes, otters, crocodiles, and turtles. More than 100 varieties water birds including storks, cranes, pelicans, eagles and more.

During the high season fueled by inflows from the Mekong, the Tonle Sap rises further with the deluges of rain that come at this time flooding the surrounding forest areas creating an abundant source of food for fish. The lake is renowned for being one of the richest fishing areas in the world. During November, water festivals are held which tie in with full moon festivals mark the end of this season and the time that flows start reversing and flowing back out the Mekong.

The lake is surrounded by five different provinces and is home to many people who live by the lake and on the lake itself. The floating villages and stilted houses have become somewhat of an attraction with it becoming a feature of the tour bus circuit. Many people are split on how to think about this but the fact is many of these people are stateless and have little or no source of income. Many who live here are of Vietnamese origin.

The key areas of Tonle Sap

Chong Neas

At about 15 km from Siem Reap it's the closest and easiest floating village to get to with boats departing the dock all day long. The boat fare is normally 20 per passenger but you'll also be presented with opportunities to part with more cash.

Unfortunately, this earns this particular spot a very dubious reputation and many leave with the feeling of being ripped off and that the locals are being used as an attraction. Rather than going to the dock and trying to haggle the boat yourself maybe try a package from https://www.facebook.com/prektoaltours/

Kampong Phluk

Home to a stilted village and flooded forest. Depending on the time you go you'll either see buildings on 6 meter high stilts (December to April) or homes sitting just above the water line (June to November). Take a boat from Chong Neas dock or in the wet season you can drive to Roulous Village and take a boat through the flooded forest to reach Kampong Phluk village.

Kompong Kleang

It's the most recommended village to visit on the lake yet, unfortunately, it's also the furtherest away. It's the largest community on the lake located some 55km from Siem Reap or about 1.5 hours by road. You can also take a boat there from Chong Neas dock. You can book package tours through https://www.kompongkhleang.org

Me Chrey

Located 25 km from Siem Reap its one of the smaller less known villages on the lake.

Ang Trapeng Thmor Reserve

One for wildlife fans the reserve is home to Sarus Crane from January to May and over 200 species of other birds. For tours see https://samveasna.org - Sam Veasna Center is a local NGO that is dedicated to conservation work and providing local communities with sustainable income through eco-tourism.

Prek Toal Bird Sanctuary

For birdwatchers, Prek Toal is the most popular spot and home to Greater and Lesser Adjutants, Black-headed Ibis, Spot-billed Pelican, Grey-Headed Fish Eagle, Painted Stork, Milky Stork, and much more. For tours visit Osmose http://www.osmosetonlesap.net

The Apsara Dance

The term Apsara comes from Hindu mythology, referring to beautiful creatures who were born from the 'Churning of the Ocean and the Milk' and were messengers of peace between heaven and earth. The Churning of the Ocean and Milk conjures up images of delicious salted ice-cream in my mind but in Hindu mythology, which was the mainstay back in the early days of the Khmer Empire, it's a part of the story in the struggle between devas (gods) and asuras (demons).

This very story of the Churning of the Ocean and Milk can be seen depicted on the southern section of the east gallery of Angkor Wat. It's one of it's most famous and beautiful bas-reliefs.

The Apsaras would perform for their earthly kings a complex dance routine leaving them mesmerized by their beauty in both form and art. During the Angkor period, it was only the kings who had the pleasure of witnessing the show and one king in particular, Jayavarman VII, liked it so much he was believed to have over three thousands of Apsara dancers in his court.

Today, we can all be kings and enjoy what is a very special and ancient traditional form of art. At first, it looks graceful but when you start to understand the story and meaning behind the movements the complexity of the dance begins to reveal itself.

The arching of the back and feet and hands throughout the dance mimics the movement of a serpentine, and important creature in mythology of the time, hand gesture and movement form to create a language that can convey a story. It's much more than a dance, understand the language and the story can flow through you as it flowed through thousands before.

There are some 300 intricate gestures (some claim there are thousands) that a fully trained Apsara dancer must learn. Students begin training as young as 9 years old and must spend years of intensive training to fully master the gestures and poses that form the language, the characters of the story, and the stories themselves. Here is a visual sample of some of those https://goo.gl/hzEVgb.

In 2003, UNESCO declared the dance a "Masterpiece of Oral and Intangible Culture" aiming to restore the tradition through funding, training, and legal protections. It is now protected by Unesco as Intangible Culture. Yet, most reports indicate that as an art form it's still suffering from low funding and development. Leading the charge and what may be a renaissance of the art form is Princess Norodom Buppha Devi and the Royal Ballet of Cambodia.

The Royal Ballet of Cambodia has recently performed in Hong Kong and is set to tour Europe in 2018.

In Siem Reap, there are a number of venues where you can enjoy a live performance by local dancers with shows held nightly as part of dinner entertainment.

Apsara Terrace - at the Raffles Grand Hotel D'Angkor is known for its impressive classical dance and martial arts performances - $46 inc Buffet - 19:00 to 21:00 - Apsara Terrace, Raffles Grand Hotel D'Angkor - http://raffles.com/siem-reap/ - 1 Vithei Charles De Gaulle Khum Svay Dang Kum

Angkor Village Apsara Theatre - https://www.angkorvillageresort.asia/apsara-theatre/ - Beautiful, elegant setting limited to 40 or so people. Apsara dance show and set menu $25. 19.30 to 21.30 - Wat Bo Rd

Kulen II Restaurant - http://www.koulenrestaurant.com - Apsara dance show and buffet offering western and Khmer cuisine $12 - Buffet starts at 6 pm and show begins at 7.30 pm. - Sivatha Blvd.

Temple Balcony - No admission fee - Apsara dance shows run continuously from 7.30 pm to 9.30 pm. Pub Street.

Smile of Angkor - http://www.smileofangkor.net - nightly buffet dinner and show in a dedicated complex. Mostly intended for Asian tour bus groups the venue sees hundreds going through its doors nightly. Dinner and show prices begin at $41. Dinner begins at 18:00 and show begins at 20:25.

The Siem Reap city center

The central city area is located some 7km from the main temple area and about 11km from the airport. It's in the central area where you will find most of the shopping, restaurant, and nightlife opportunities.

Sivatha Boulevard is the main thoroughfare which runs north to south and along here you can find lots of massage shops, small restaurants, hotels, travel agents, supermarkets and much more.

Sok San Road is developing all the time and features the new Temple Container Pub Zone, Hip Hop Club, and Temple Cafe development. The road is lined either side for almost it's entire length with cafes, restaurants, small bars and massage shops.

Along Preah Sangreach Tep Vong St you'll find from west to east, Chao Sang Hok supermarket, Asia Market, numerous restaurants, Roma Pizza, Naga Guest House, the Park Hyatt and once it crosses Sivatha Blvd there is an ABA Bank, tourist shops, Royal ANZ bank, Cellcard store, Thai Hout supermarket and Kandal Village.

On Wat Bo Road you'll find many guest houses, hotels, restaurants, Gloria Jeans and BioLab cafe, and a few more massage places.

National Road 6, or NR6, or Highway 6, or if you like, Airport Road, in the western direction heads to the airport and beyond that Poipet, in the eastern direction it heads to Phnom Penh. Along the city section of the road you'll find lots of the large tour group hotels, Cambodian Cultural Village, Senteurs D Angkor, Wat Kesararam, Brown Coffee and heading east there is Phsar Leu Market.

This map on the next page will help you get a rough bearing.

The four main roads are National Road 6 (NR6) which leads to Phnom Penh in one direction and Poipet in the other, Sivatha Blvd which is the central thoroughfare, Pokambor Ave, Charles De Guille aka temple road, and Wat Bo Road. Online Map: https://goo.gl/5eibLQ

50

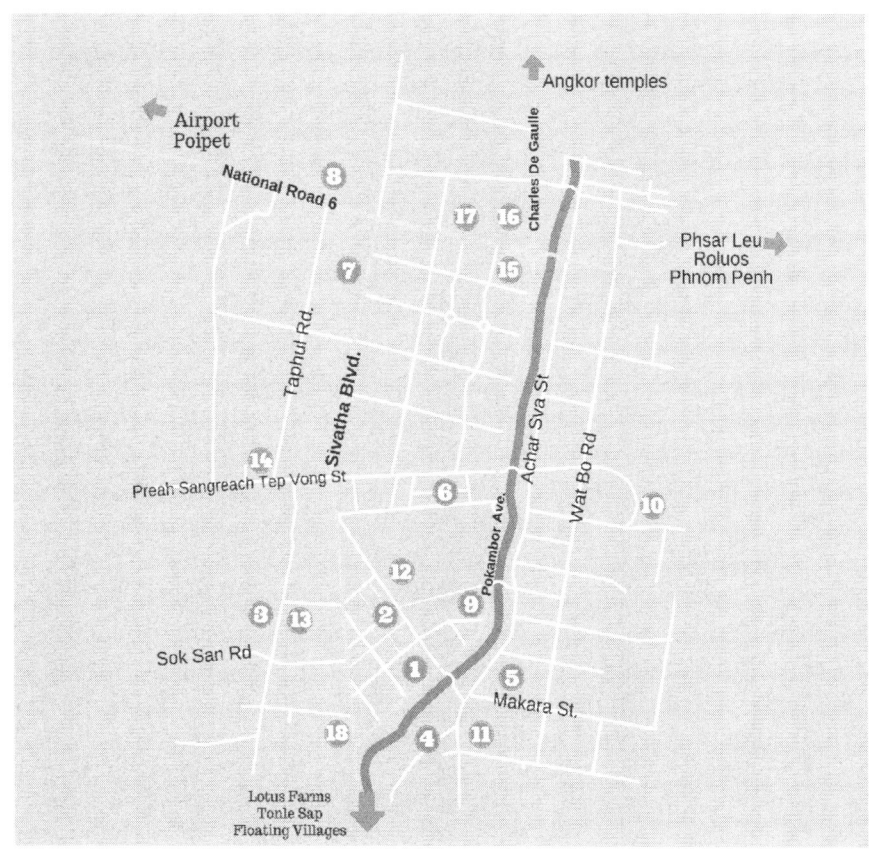

1. Old Market 2. Pub Street 3. Angkor Night Market 4. Art Centre Night Market 5. Kings Road/Made in Cambodia Market 6. Kandall Village 7. Lucky Mall 8. Wat Kesararam 9. Wat Preah Prohm Rath 10. Wat Bo 11. Wat Damnak 12. Provincial Hospital 13. Noon Night Market 14. Asia Market (supermarket) 15. Royal Palace 16. Royal Gardens 17. Prea Ang Chek, Ang Chorm & Neak Ta 18. Platinum Complex

The Pub Street and Old Market Area

1. Old Market shops 2. Wet Market and Veg 3 & 4. Various touristy shops and street stalls 5. Noi Coffee 6. Angkor Trade Centre 7. New Leaf Eatery 8. U Care Pharmacy 9. Ankgor What? Bar 10. Temple Club & Balcony 11. The Piano 12. Temple Bar 13. Cheers bar 14. Yolo bar 15. X- Bar 16. The Triangle Bar and BB Market 17. Ten Bells restaurant 18. Platinum Cineplex 19. Miss Wong bar and restaurant 20. Asana restaurant and bar 21. Siem Reap Night Market 22. Reggae Bar 23. Chamkar Vegetarian Online Map: https://goo.gl/5eibLQ

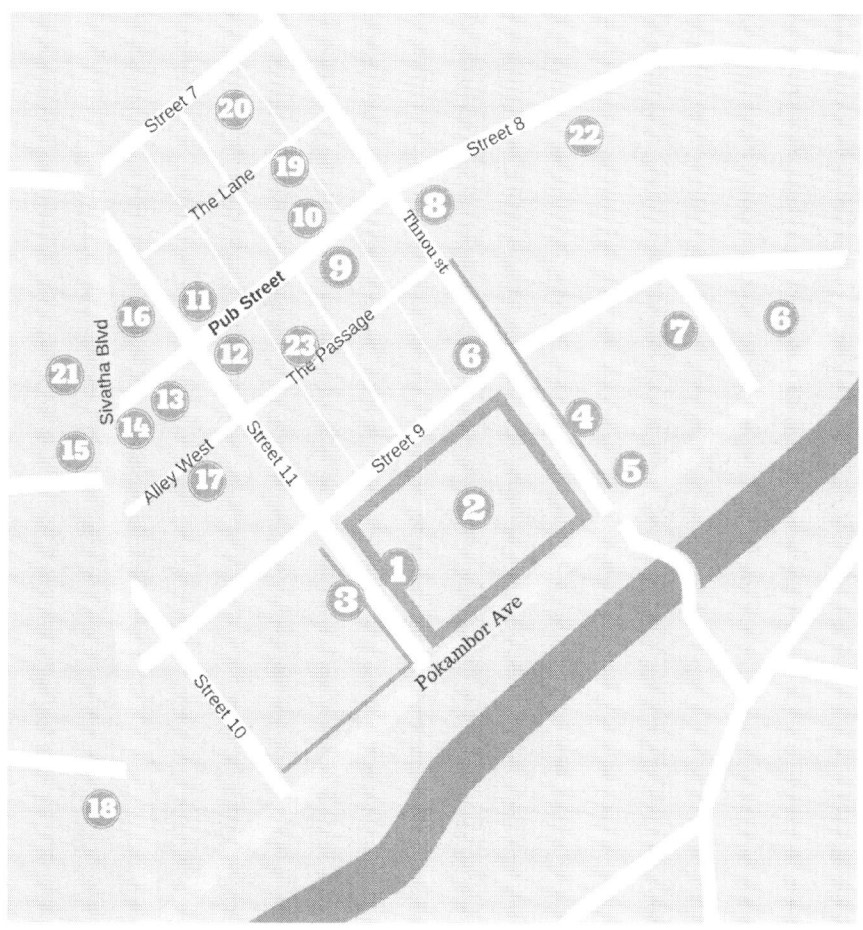

What to eat and where

Of course, the most popular area for eating and drinking is the Pub Street area which sprawls across several streets containing numerous restaurants. The food prices here range from $5-10 for a meal and to the rejoice of every sweaty visitor, beers start at a mere 50 cents.

For most travelers, the Pub Street area is convenient with everything in one area, it's clean, and tailored to overseas visitors. You'll have no trouble finding Italian, Indian, Korean, French, Western and other cuisines along with local Khmer dishes.

For the most part, I am going to focus on the local cuisine. Cambodian cuisine shares similarities with Thailand while taking influences from China, Vietnam and even it's old colonial masters, the French.

Local must-try dishes in Siem Reap

1. Sangvak - small portions of ground fish are baked in banana leaves and served with raw vegetables, fresh herbs, Khmer noodles, and a dipping sauce. Simply put the fish cake together with some noodles, and some herb leaves then wrap it in lettuce or cabbage and dip and eat.

2. Amok - a curry that is available with either fish or chicken as the protein. Fish is the most popular and its ingredients include coconut milk, lemongrass, turmeric, garlic, shallots, galangal, and ginger. Served with rice it's very mild sometimes bordering on sweet. Local chefs have a tendency to burn the garlic which in my belief destroys the dish, find a good one and you'll love this dish.

3. Lok Lak - Beef (or Chicken) in a pepper sauce. Often served with veggies, and in the more westernized restaurants, it's served with tomato slices, lettuce, and fries. Simple dish but it can be a bit hit and miss with the beef often being too chewy. Get a good one and you'll be sure to enjoy it.

4. Banh Chiao - a savory crepe that's filled with ground pork and bean sprouts.

5. Nom Banh Chok - Khmer noodles - thin rice noodles are

immersed in a sweet green curry featuring kaffir lime leaves, mint leaves, bean sprouts, lemongrass, and turmeric.

6. Lap Khmer - A cold salad featuring lime marinated beef that's only lightly seared, or sometimes raw, along with lemongrass, shallots, garlic, local basil, mint, green beans, green pepper and red chili.

7. Neorm Svye Kchey - A salad combining a protein either fish or shrimp, along with mango, cashews, carrot, basil and a Khmer dressing that combines fish sauce, lime juice, and palm sugar.

8. Naem - a spring roll that's packed with fresh veg. Recipes differ but you'll find herbs, carrot, lettuce, cucumber and maybe rice noodle inside paired with a peanut dipping sauce.

Where to eat

You can find local cuisine in an around Pub Street but for a more genuine local experience find your favorite Tuk-Tuk driver and head to the market on Road 60 which fires up late afternoon. Here you will find locals picnicking by the roadside, market stalls with very cheap clothes and accessories, and 'plastic chair' restaurants that serve up local favorites where you'll spend no more than a few dollars for a fair feast. You could also head out about 15 mins towards Tonle Sap to the huts set among the lotus fields. Some have English menus and it's particularly beautiful when the lotus flowers are in bloom. The bamboo huts catch the breeze quite nicely and are fitted out with hammocks to relax in after you have filled yourself silly. Again, for these ones, tag your favorite tuk-tuk driver and they'll know where to go.

In the Pub Street you won't be able to miss the big players in the area being the **Red Piano**, **Temple Bar** and **Triangle Bar**. They are almost icons of Siem Reap having served tourists flocking in and out of the area for longer than I know. The area is going through somewhat of a revival with many cool hipster cafes and fusion restaurants coming in with modern decor. You'll have no trouble spotting those so there's no need for me to say more except to say be sure to take a peek down the laneways. The laneways are very charismatic packed with eateries and the odd gift shop making for a chic place to hang and get some selfies if you must.

For local cuisine in Pub Street try **Le Tigre de Papier** - http://letigredepapier.com - cozy little restaurant bar that has local and western cuisines. They also offer cooking classes. Street 08 (Eastern end of Pub Street). Wander to the Old Market and at the corner of Thnou St and Street 9, you'll find **Khmer Kitchen** - http://www.khmerkitchens.com - offering local dishes at fair prices. Across the road, in the Old Market on Street 9, you'll find **Nai Khmer Restaurant** where you can sit side by side with locals and enjoy local cuisine and great prices.

If the hustle and bustle of Pub Street is not your thing, try heading down Sok San Road where you'll find several really laid back, open cafe/restaurants that are clean, comfy and serve up great food. Prices are a little cheaper too. A couple of highlights of the street are **Kuriosity Cafe** - https://kuriositykafe.com - which serves local dishes along with western options in a cafe/bistro setting featuring some modern retro/movie inspired deco and across the road is **Villa Sok San** which offers great value. Also, take a stroll along the Angkor Night Market Street that heads north to south. At its northern end after the Night Market you'll find **Rom Chang Khmer Restaurant** which is clean and serves great value local and western food, and a little further along the popular **Bugs Cafe** - http://bugs-cafe.e-monsite.com - where you can try culinary creations featuring crickets, scorpions, spiders, ants and more.

Head along Preah Sangreach Tep Vong St and you'll find Naga Guest House which is followed by several good value eateries. Many are the basic plastic chair and stainless steel table restaurants but if you will find tasty food at a fair price. There is also a wood-fired pizza bar with great prices on that same street. Head up Taphul Road towards the intersection with Oum Khun St and you'll find several small cafes catering to western style Cambodian food with prices ranging from $1 to $4. A recommendation on that street is **Bong Srey Mith Laor** at the corner of Taphul Road and Oum Khun St that makes the best omelets in town served with a baguette, salad, and fresh coffee for the grand sum of $2 along with a range of western and local dishes for lunch and dinner.

On the other side of the river try **Cuisine Wat Damnak** - http://www.cuisinewatdamnak.com - which offers upscale French Cambodian fusion (near Angkor High School) with prices for multi-course meal experience ranging from 5 courses for $27 or 6 courses for $31. Nearby on Street 24 you'll find **Square 24** - http://www.thesquare24.com/ - another modern fine Khmer dining experience with the two stand out choices being their two Khmer set menu choices offering 6 courses from $16. If you are looking for something in that area that's a bit easier on the hip pocket try **Khmer Grill** - http://www.khmergrill.com - located on Watdamnak Road offers traditional BBQ and local dishes. Nearby there is another recommended choice, **Geneieve's** - https://www.facebook.com/GenevievesRestaurant/ - Khmer Asian cuisine and best of all they plow a lot back into the community, find them on Bamboo Street. Another suggestion in the area is **Chong Phov Khmer Restaurant** – https://www.facebook.com/KhmerStaffMeals/ - which offers authentic local dishes and lovely landscaped surrounds on Sombai Road.

Out towards the temples, you can find **Marum** - http://tree-alliance.org/our-restaurants/marum.php - superb modern Khmer cuisine with a feel-good bonus as it's run by an NGO that supports marginalised children in Siem Reap. Located near Wot Polanka. Nearby you'll find **Mie Cafe** - http://www.miecafe-siemreap.com - set within a traditional wooden Khmer house and garden it offers modern Khmer cuisine prepared by a Swiss-trained Cambodian chef.

Other Recommended cafes in Siem Reap

Also see the section on Coffee and Co-Working Spaces

Peace Cafe - http://www.peacecafeangkor.org - vegetarian cafe in a peaceful garden setting. Also offering cooking classes ' East River Road, Siem Reap

Sister Srey Cafe - http://www.sistersreycafe.com - popular place focussed on fresh, healthy food ' 200 Pokambor St, Old Market Area

New Leaf Eatery - https://newleafeatery.com - Locally sourced and roasted coffee, a full menu of western and local ' No. 306 Street 9

Little Red Fox Espresso - http://thelittleredfoxespresso.com - Hup Guan Street (Kandal Village)

The Hive - https://facebook.com/thehive.siemreap - Australian-inspired brunch - Psar Kandal Street (Central Market Street)

Other recommended restaurants

Miss Wong - http://misswong.net - step back into 1930s Shanghai and sip on fine cocktails and classic dim sum, hot pot and more - The Lane, Pub Street Area, Siem Reap

Brothers & Brothers Plus - http://www.thebrotherscambodia.com - amazing value and always delicious. Local Khmer and western dishes - 7 Makara Road (Kings Road)

L'Annexe - https://www.annexesiemreap.com - Traditional French cuisine in a lush garden setting. Great value - Sok San Road

Maharajah - https://www.facebook.com/Royal.Indian/ - Indian restaurant with vegetarian and no-vegetarian options. Sivatha Road Old Market Area, Front Of Terrasse Des Elephants

The Hashi Japanese Restaurant - http://www.thehashi.com - upmarket Japanese dining including a Sushi bar. Wat Bo Road near Gloria Jeans

Chamkar Vegetarian Restaurant - The only dedicated vegetarian restaurant in the Pub Street area, and it's a good one. Located in the Passageway.

Western Fast Food

KFC - Sivatha Blvd

Burger King - Sivatha Blvd

Dinner and show

Angkor Village Apsara Theatre - https://www.angkorvillageresort.asia/apsara-theatre/ - Beautiful, elegant setting limited to 40 or so people. Apsara dance show and set menu $25. 7.30-9.30 - Wat Bo Rd

Kulen II Restaurant - http://www.koulenrestaurant.com - Apsara dance show and buffet offering western and Khmer cuisine $12 - Buffet starts at 6 pm and show begins at 7.30 pm. - Sivatha Blvd.

Apsara Terrace - http://www.raffles.com/siem-reap/dining/the-apsara-terrace/ - Pan Asian buffet and one of the most highly rated shows in Siem Reap. $45 for adults with discounts for Children. Buffet begins at 7 and show at 7.45 pm. - 1 Vithei Charles de Gaulle.

Temple Balcony - No admission fee - Apsara dance shows run continuously from 7.30pm to 9.30pm. Pub Street.

Eat for a Cause

Haven - http://www.havencambodia.com - Asian-Western fusion with a mix of the healthy and classic comfort foods. Haven also operates as a training center giving underprivileged and vulnerable youth valuable skills to carry them through life - Chocolate Rd, Wat Damnak area

Blossom Cafe - http://www.blossomcakes.org - Delicious cupcakes and more. Students are referred to the program by different organizations and then trained on-site receiving skills for life. - 6 Mondul 1 Svay Dangkum

Sala Bai Hotel School - http://www.salabai.com/restaurant-salabai.php - Their training restaurant serves a set menu prepared by students with the income supporting the training costs. Open weekdays for breakfast and lunch. - located 5 mins out of town off road 63, near Wat Svay.

Buffet Breakfast Anyone?

If your hotel or hostel hasn't something to offer I have a couple of excellent suggestions for you.

Grill Wine Cafe at Memoire Boutique Hotel - http://www.grillwinecafe.com - offers a comfortable setting with a full buffet breakfast including eggs cooked to preference, fresh noodles, congee, bacon, fresh bread and pastries, drinks and more. Eat as much as you like for $7.70 - 07.00 to 10.00 - 54 Sivattha Blvd (near Lucky Mall)

Malis Restaurant - https://www.malis-restaurant.com - a fusion of local and western cuisines in a very beautiful restaurant offering free-flow breakfast. Anything on the menu and as much as you like which includes croissants, eggs to order, local dishes such as nom banh chok, coffee, and fresh juices. - $7 - 06.30 to 10.30 - Pokambor Street (near to the intersection of Central Market St)

Damrei Angkor Hotel - http://www.damreiangkorhotel.com - hotel buffet breakfast that is also open to outside guests. Mix of Asian and Western at a fantastic price. - $4 - Street 20

Local foods and fruits

Cambodia shares a number of fruits and vegetables that are popular throughout Asia which you may find unique, and several in the class of superfoods.

1. Koulen (Lychee) - small round with a red rough textured flesh that's peeled away to reveal the white flesh of the fruit. Lychee contains good quantities of iron, magnesium, copper, vitamin C, manganese, and folate, along with having high concentrations of polyphenols.

2. Meangkhout (Mangosteen) - The red, almost black in color, thick skin is broken away to reveal a beautiful snow white segmented flesh that is sweet and delicious. Best eaten in season. The fruit is rich in fiber, Vitamin C, Vitamin B, copper, manganese, magnesium, and potassium.

3. Mean (Longnan) - a light beige thin crisp skin is peeled away to reveal sweet white flesh. The nutritional profile is very similar to Lychee.

4. Khnol (Jackfruit) - Popular throughout Asia, you'll often see Jackfruit being sold by the roadside out of small trucks. Quite large with a hard light green spiky skin that's peeled away to reveal a sweet bright yellow flesh.

5. Saray (Asian pear) - Light beige/yellow skin contains a flesh that's something between an apple and a pear.

6. Kampot Pepper - Grown in the Kampot Province, and only there, it is renowned as the world's finest pepper, at least by the French. There are three types being, white, red and black. You'll see it in little packets at touristy shops everywhere. The best place to buy is Starling Farm Kampot Pepper on Street 7.

7. Moringa - a green leafy plant that grows throughout Asia, this is a super super food. A quick intro into its amazing qualities are that it has 2 x the protein of yogurt, 4 x the vitamin A of carrots, 3 x the potassium of bananas, 4 x the calcium of milk and 7 x the vitamin C of oranges. Some supermarkets such as Chao Sang Hok sell powdered forms of Moringa, there is a also a stall at Made in Cambodia Market (Kings Road), I Dig Herbs, selling Moringa Powder and other locally made teas etc..

8.Tearb Barung (Soursop) - The dark green spiky outer skin reveals a flesh that's creamy with a taste like a mashing of strawberry and pineapple. It's high in antioxidants and has been claimed as a cancer-fighting food, able to fight infections and reduce degenerative eye diseases.

9. Rambutan - an oval-shaped fruit with red skin coarsely covered in red 'hairs'. Peel the skin away to reveal the super sweet white flesh. The fruit is high in carbohydrates, fats, proteins, iron, phosphorus, vitamin C and also calcium.

10. Tolep (Persimmon) - Persimmon is orange in color and somewhat similar to a tomato. High in vitamin A along with containing vitamin c, b-complex vitamins, manganese, phosphorous and copper.

11. Romdeng (Galangal) - very similar to ginger and also has similar medical properties such as being claimed as an anti-inflammatory.

12. Terk dos ko (Milk Fruit) - A greenish, purplish skin that's not eaten holds a juicy, sweet, jelly-like flesh.

Shopping

Most of the shopping opportunities are centered around Pub Street/Old Market area and along Sivatha Blvd. There is also a cluster of large warehouse-style stores and T Galleria as you head out towards Angkor, mostly these are designed for large tour groups with many catering especially to Chinese and Korean groups. You may find T Galleria interesting if you are in the market for genuine luxury brand goods.

Markets

Angkor Night Market - http://angkornightmarket.com - local wares, paintings, crafts and lots of t-shirts and clothes - 16.00 to 24.00 - Off Sivatha Boulevard and then along Angkor Night Market Road.

Noon Market - Smaller market but jam-packed, similar items to other markets. Located opposite Angkor Night Market in the lane that connects Sivatha Blvd to Angkor Night Market road.

Siem Reap Night Market - Located on Sivatha Blvd opposite the Triangle Bar, offering mostly clothes, prices are fair and there is also a stage here where they have a nightly "Lady Boy Show" satire performance.

Siem Reap Art Centre Night Market - located along the riverside it offers much the same goods as the other markets. Can be much more relaxed than other markets, and prices may be a little cheaper- 16.00 to 22.00 - Across the river from Old Market.

Old Market (Psar Chas) - traditional Cambodian market at its center with tourist shops around the outer perimeter selling local wares and lots of clothes - 07.00 to 20.00 - Psar Chaa Road

Full Moon Night Market - https://www.facebook.com/fullmoonnightmarketandrestaurant/ - a smaller market with mostly touristy t-shirts - 09.00 to 24.00 - Sivatha Road near Lucky Mall.

BB Angkor Market - at the entry to Pub Street beneath the Triangle Bar there-s a cluster of market stalls flogging silverware, t-shirts and elephant pants.

Made in Cambodia Market - https://www.facebook.com/MadeinCambodiaMarket/ - this market area has a much more relaxed feel, with the market stalls nestled amongst several cafes and restaurants it-s a comfortable place to hang - 12.00 to 22.00 - Kings Road.

China Tang Market - handicrafts, souvenirs, factory outlet clothing, cosmetics, and jewelers - Sivatha Blvd opposite Pub Street.

Road 60 Market - mostly goods for locals, but cheap. Great place to try out genuine local food - Opens in the afternoon closing late - Road 60 just past the Angkor Ticket Office.

Psar Leu Market - you could call it the local version of WalMart, it-s a massive traditional local market and has everything locals need and use in their daily life. Wet Market, vegetables, hardware, DIY, homewares, jewelry, clothes and fashion, and much more. You might not buy anything here but it is a worthy exploration of a hub of local daily life - 06.00 to 18.00 - National Road 6.

Malls

T Galleria by DFS - International Chinese mall chain, designed for Chinese tourists. It-s modern and is packed with luxury brands - 968 Vithei Charles De Gaulle, Krong Siem Reap

Angkor Shopping Arcade - 09.00 to 22.00 - 968 Vithei Charles De Gaulle.

Lucky Mall - http://luckymarketgroup.com - is the most popular and visit Mall in Siem Reap. The Mall has a huge supermarket on the ground floor which has a wide range of local and imported products - 09.00 to 22.00 - Sivatha Boulevard near to Highway 6.

Angkor Trade Center - featuring international restaurant chains, entertainment, and supermarket - 09.00 to 21.00 - Cnr of Street 9 and Pokambor Avenue.

Angkor Fashion Plaza – https://www.facebook.com/AFP.AngkorFashionPlaza - a modern department store featuring genuine brand name lines such as

Nike, Adidas, Under Armour and more, with prices at full retail, on the upstairs floor there is some value and they do occasionally have sales – Cnr of Achar Sva St and Street 20

Local Crafts

Artisans d-Angkor/Pouk Silk Farm - http://artisansdangkor.com - learn about local silk production and textiles - 08.00 to 17.30 - Located in Pouk district, 20 minutes from Siem Reap. There is also an Artisans d-Angkor near the pub street area on Steung Thmei st.

Khmer Ceramics Centre - http://khmerceramics.com - Traditional Cambodian craftsmanship, classes also available - #130, Vithey Charles de Gaulle (Temple Road)

Made in Cambodia Market - https://www.facebook.com/MadeinCambodiaMarket/ - handicrafts, souvenirs, performances, cafes, and restaurants - 12.00 to 22.00 - Kings Road.

Angkor Handicraft Association - http://aha-kh.com - certified locally made goods including handmade silk, cotton, silverware, statues, bronze and wood, hand-woven textiles, paintings, bags and accessories, ceramics and much more - 10.00 to 19.00 - Road 60, Trang Village, Sangkat Slorkram Commune

Senteurs d-Angkor - http://www.senteursdangkor.com - Soaps are all made by hand, using local raw materials, traditional techniques and extracts derived exclusively from plant oils and 100 % natural ingredients. You can visit their workshop and watch the artisans at work - 8:00 am - 5:30 pm (every day) - NR 6 (Near to Angkor Palace Resort). There is also a store opposite old market on the hospital road.

Angkor Recycled - https://www.angkorrecycled.org - Handmade bags, purses and wallets, all created from recycled products that are collected locally helping to clean the environment, and handcrafted by locals who are the end beneficiaries.

Theams House - http://theamshouse.com - locally produced arts and crafts by renowned local artist Lim Muy Theam and his team. You can watch items being created before your eyes and purchase something very local and very unique. 25 Veal Village

Kandal Village

An emerging shopping and dining area set amongst the old French quarter that features a range of boutique fashion stores, cafes and coffee shops. The area is bordered by Sivatha Blvd, Tep Vong St, Central Market St and Pokambort Ave. Highlights include Neary Khmer Angkor Shop for locally made silks and tailors, Shop 676 for male and female fashions made from natural fibers, Bloom Cafe, Little Red Fox Espresso, The Hive (cafe), and much more.

Groceries

Asia Market - has two locations, with a store on Sivatha Rd near Central Market St (8.00 to 24.00) and a new store on the corner of Preah Sangreach Tep Vong St and Taphul Rd (open 24hrs). Good range with many imported lines but some items can be found elsewhere much cheaper.

Angkor Market - possibly one of the most popular supermarkets, featuring a good range of products including imported lines. Cheeses, dairy, and some meats. Upstairs has a large range of household needs. Breathe in as you walk around the isles! - 07.00 to 22.00 - Cnr of Sivatha Blvd. and Oum Khun St.

Thai Huot - http://www.thaihuot.com - Large range with many imported lines and quite reasonable prices. Also, has bulk lots. Lots of cheeses, dairy and imported meats. Preah Sangreach Tep Vong St near to the river.

Lucky Supermarket - http://luckymarketgroup.com - Good range with fair prices. Probably the best range of fresh food along with the nearby Angkor Market - 09.00 to 21.00 - Inside Lucky Mall on Sivatha Blvd.

Chao Sang Hok - on Preah Sangreach Tep Vong St near to Funky Flashpacker. Good range and cheap prices on common lines. Also, has a store on National Road 6.

Triangle Market - http://facebook.com/Triangle-Market - at the corner of National Highway 6 and Sivatha Blvd, it-s a handy stop to grab a few things as you head out to the temples.

Metro Market - http://facebook.com/metromarketcambodia/ - on Sivatha Blvd opposite the High School and near to Mad Monkey Hostel.

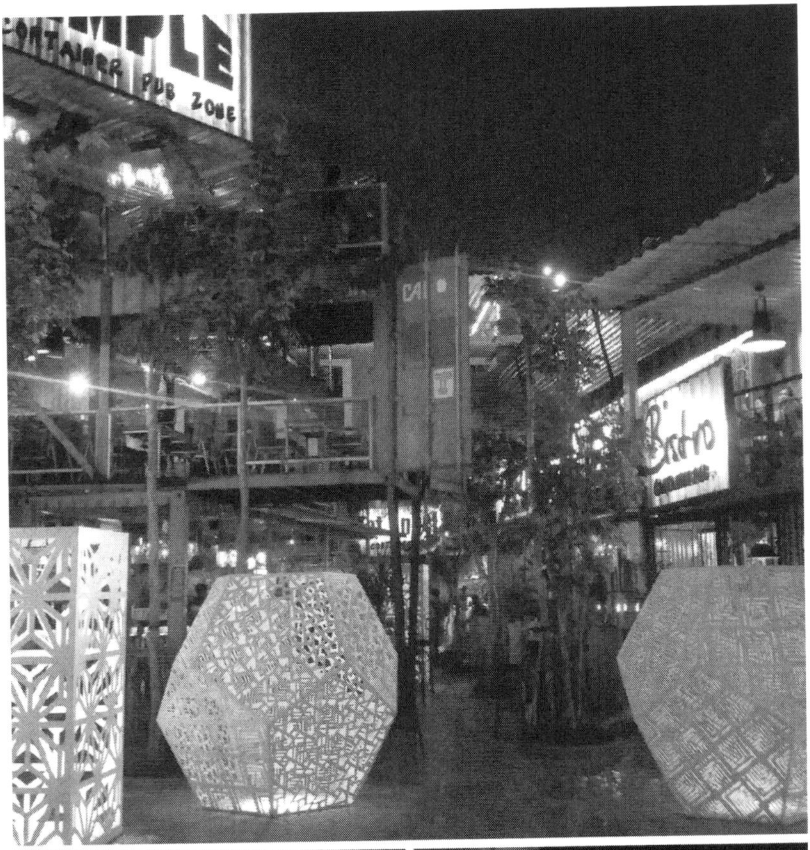
CONTAINER PUB ZONE

UB STREET

CAFÉ CENTRAL
POLIAKOV
MARTINI

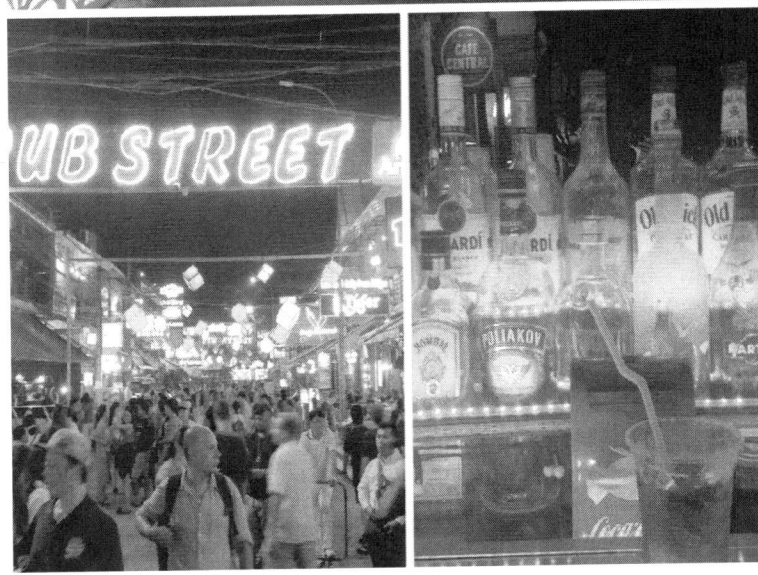

Nightlife

At the core of nightlife in Siem Reap is Pub Street with its 50 cent beers and happy hours with 1.50 mojitos. The area begins the night in very family friendly mode until the later hours when it morphs into a fully fledged party zone with clubs in full swing and mobile pop-up bars occupy the streets.

The two most popular clubs are **Temple Club** and **Angkor What** which are in the heart of Pub Street directly opposing each other. Angkor What opens as a bar at 2 pm and morphs into a club with a DJ mixing classics and latest pop until closing time around 4 pm. If you get bored with that, the Temple Club across the road, which serves meals during the day in one section with an alfresco area out front, offers a nightclub downstairs and a rooftop lounge bar upstairs for something a little more chilled.

The **Red Piano** has 50 cent beers all day and night, and **Triangle Bar** has 50 cent beers downstairs and nightly live bands upstairs, opposite Triangle Bar you'll find **Cheers** which is an open fronted bar/nightclub. Besides that, you can head upstairs to the **YOLO bar** which seems to be targeting younger backpackers.

Early in the night mobile popup bars will congregate around the old market and after 11 pm they will fill the area outside of Cheers. They are not to be missed, some are nothing more than a frame mounted on top of Honda moto with a couple of speakers hanging off the sides and a few flashing lights, some are far more elaborate. Grab a mojito or your favorite cocktail for a great discount on bar prices, pick your favorite hits on their laptop and swing it street style.

How about a half-pipe, pool tables and DJ at a rooftop bar? That's **XBar**, located at the start of Sok San Road and looking down along Pub Street. Opening at 3 pm, it usually starts to fire up around 10 pm and closes as the sun comes up around 6 am.

Keep heading down Sok San Road and you'll find a large modern **Score Sports Bar & Grill** which has live music on weekends and is fairly laid back and never too crazy. If you are looking to mingle with locals, keep going down Sok San Road and you'll find the new **Temple Container Pub Zone** and **Classic Hip Hop**

Club. It's a new development which features bistro, bar, and the attached nightclub that's very popular with the young local crowd.

Also along Sok San Road you'll find numerous smaller bars offering friendly personal service and ice cold drinks which are great if your looking for something more laid back than the Pub Street scene.

Something more refined? Head to **Miss Wongs** in the laneway beside Pub Street for superb cocktails in a chic 60's Shanghai environment, or try **G-Green Sky Dining** on the top of the Platinum Complex for rooftop views and cocktails. Another spot in the central area is **Asana**, enter off Street 7, offers up rustic charm and cocktails in one of the last traditional Khmer wooden houses left in the central area.

Outside of the pub street area Martini fans looking for a quiet spot will surely love the **Martini Lounge** at Belmond La Residence d'Angkor on East River Road.

How about local brews?

Yes, you can. Head to Siem Reap Brew Pub, the city's only brewery offering 5 different boutique brews which are best to acquainted with via their sampler set offer. http://www.siemreapbrewpub.asia - corner of street 5 and 14.

Rooftop Bars

A great way to take in the sunset and beautiful nighttime atmosphere, there are several places to check out.

Temple Sky Lounge - with pool, live music stage, beanbags it's super relaxed place to be. Temple Bakery Cafe on Achar Sva St.

Temple Balcony - similar to Sky Lounge with pool and bean bags it also has live Apsara Dance shows between 7.30 and 9.30 followed by DJ's till 4 am.

X Bar - open air rooftop bar with DJ, pool tables, and a half-pipe - Sok San Road

G-Green Sky Dining - rooftop bar and restaurant on top of the Platinum Cinema complex. Sivatha Blvd.

Happy Hours

Everybody loves happy hours, and there's no shortage of them in Siem Reap, actually, I doubt there's a bar that doesn't have a sign with "happy hour" on it. Here are some picks:

Hard Rock Cafe - the prices are hefty, so happy hour is the time to go - 7-10pm - Kings Road

Longs Bar - hip place with happy hour from 5-7pm - Pub Street in the north-south laneway between The Lane and Street 7

Peace and Love - 50 cent beer and $1 cocktails from 3-8pm

Soul Train Reggae Bar - happy hour from 4-8pm - Little Pub Street

The Ten Bells - happy hour from 5-7pm - Alley West

Swimming Pools and Gyms

Most hotels and even hostels will have a pool and I urge to you use, but, I am sure after a long day at the temples you won't need any incentive to jump in and cool down.

No pool? Don't worry, there are plenty of options. Nearly all hotels make their pools open to the public for a small fee and many also include gym and sauna, so here are a few suggestions.

Prince d'Angkor - http://www.princedangkor.com - a four-star hotel on Sivatha Boulevard, features a large salt water pool and access includes gym. - $8 - Sivatha Blvd

Angkor Century Hotel - http://www.angkorcentury.com - very large pool and entry price includes gym and steam/sauna. - $8 - Komay Road

Somadevi Resort & Spa - http://www.somadeviangkor.com - nice size pool with gym, jacuzzi, sauna access - $8 - Sivatha Blvd

Angkor Dynasty Water Park - https://www.facebook.com/angkordynasty/ - a newly opened water park, and in the future a cultural theme park and shopping area, features a wave pool, water slides, kids pool, large screen and more. - $8 - Charles De Guille (Angkor Wat Road)

Something cheaper? Try Jeanies on Sok San Road where you can swim for free with any food or drink purchase, likewise with the nearby Villa Sok San.

And if you see a nice pool somewhere, just head in and ask as nearly all places open their pools to the public for a small fee.

Workout time?

The three hotels listed above also have gyms but if you are looking for a dedicated gym try these

Mr Ly Gym - https://www.facebook.com/lygym/ - One of the most popular in Siem Reap also stocking a range of supplements and also offering personal training, kick boxing classes and more. - 06:00 - 20:30 - $1 - Bakeng Road

Angkor Muscle Gym - https://www.facebook.com/Angkor-

Muscle-Gym-1420178121529234/ - 06:00 - 21:00 - $1.50 - South of Wat Damnak

Kool Apartments Gym - https://www.facebook.com/apartmentsiemreap/ - 08.00 to 20.00 - $2.50 with pool - NR6 near Red Crab Restaurant

Angkor InterFitness Gym - http://www.angkorinterfitness.com - perhaps the most modern and comfortable offering a range of services inc. Yoga, Zumba, Pilates, Crossfit, Cardio, Kick Boxing and personal training. They also have steam and sauna. - 06.00 to 21.00 - $5 - Tep Vong St above Thai Hout Supermarket

Coffee Shops and Co-Working Spaces

Looking for a great coffee, a comfortable chair, air-con, and WiFi? Me too, always! here is a list of some of the places that you-d find me staring a laptop screen.

Gloria Jeans - Wat Bo Road - http://gloriajeans.com.kh - There are two Gloria Jeans shops in SR, this particular one is on Wat Bo Road. Its spacious, clean, comfy and cool with fast wifi. If you like a latte with perfectly steamed milk, try here. Near the intersection of street 22 and Wat Bo Road.

Brown Coffee - https://browncoffee.com.kh - Modern, large, open, it's a bit of an oasis with great coffee, good food, and fair prices, unfortunately, only limited seats have access to power - NR6 and Taphul Rd

Bio Lab - http://biolabcafe.com - great lattes at a very fair price ($1.60). The perfect place for Digital Nomads offering plenty of power sockets, seating, and fast dependable wifi. Across the road from Gloria Jeans Coffee on Wat Bo Road.

Brother Bong - https://www.facebook.com/brotherbongcafe/ - Superb latte ($2), great comfort food such as ham and cheese toasties along with service with a smile. Recommended. Located on Funky Lane near to Funky Flashpacker.

Little Red Fox Espresso - http://www.thelittleredfoxespresso.com - Superb latte ($2.75) in a cozy environment, gets busy here. Hap Guan St, Kandal Village

The Missing Socks Laundry Cafe - https://www.facebook.com/themissingsocks/ - cozy little cafe, that's clean and a bit hip. Great coffee and delicious comfort food. Bonus, they also have washing machines and dryers where you can do a load while you enjoy the coffee, food, and wifi. 55 Steung Thmei, Svaydangkum Village (just off Sok San road).

Temple Coffee n Bakery - the Temple group is ubiquitous across the pub street with multiple cafes, bars, restaurants and massage centers. Their new cafe is just across the river from the pub street area and it-s a good one. Decent meals for $3-$9 and drinks from $1.50. It-s spacious and on the second level you'll find lounge beds/chairs (with nearby power) and there's also a Skylounge on the third floor. Coffee can be hit and miss. Achar Sva St.

Coffee Bean and Tea Leaf - http://coffeebean.com.kh - clean with comfy seats, air-con, with most seats have access to power. Note: prices here have recently gone up and the coffee is no match for other places on this list. - #073-076, Street Hospital Sangkat #2, Svay Dangkum (near pub street)

Co-working Spaces

Digital nomads looking for somewhere to plug-in might also try these:

Angkor Hub - https://angkorhub.com

1961 - http://the1961.com

Lub'd - https://www.lubd.com/siemreap/

ATMs and Money in Siem Reap

The main currency in use is the US dollar including 1, 5, 10, 20, 50 and 100 dollar notes. You may come across 2 dollar notes and I advise to not accept these as most other people won't if you do get stuck with some don't fret as major stores and banks will happily accept them.

Small change is returned in local currency, the Riel, and just keep in mind 1000 Riel is 25 cents, 2000 Riel is 50 cents and 4000 Riel = 1USD.

The local Reil comes in notes denominated 100, 500, 1000, 2000 and 10,000 reil.

ATMs are everywhere, the most popular being those from the ABA bank. Much like any other ATM, slide your card in, select language, enter your pin and choose your account and amount you'd like to withdraw. You are asked if you want a receipt, always say yes! Your card will come out first then take your cash.

Note that there is a fee for withdrawals, which varies with the amount you withdraw, as an example for $100 it's a hefty $4.

At some ATMs, you can choose between the local Reil and USD, choose USD, for if you withdraw $300 in Reil that's 1,200,000 Reil and you'll better have a wheelbarrow to carry it!

Continuing with that example and withdrawing your $300 in USD, you'll get 3 x 100 dollar bills which are next to useless as no shop can handle giving change for that amount. You can try withdrawing $290 let's say, which will give you $90 worth of usable notes. Use the 100 dollar bills for large purchases or exchange them at the money changer (and pay another fee!) or go into the bank and they will change it for you.

The most useful notes to carry are 1, 5, 10 and 20.

You can search Google Maps for ABA ATM locations, they are dark green in color and similar in style to phone boxes and located everywhere. If I was making 4 bucks a withdrawal, I would put them everywhere too! The main branch office is located on Tep Vong St.

Another note about ATMs, always select to get a receipt, I have heard several people complain about not getting any money after making a withdrawal which was rectified on visiting the main branch.

Other banks include Maybank with an office and ATM on Sivatha Blvd, Royal ANZ with several ATMs around the city area and an office on Tep Vong St, Canadia Bank with a few ATMs in main areas, Bank of China with a branch and ATM at the intersection of NR6 and Sivatha Blvd.

Important - Always check your change, for if you get a torn note or damaged note, no one will accept it.

Some larger upmarket stores and restaurants, some hotels and select supermarkets will accept credit cards but for the most part, you'll be using cash everywhere.

Beating the Heat

Cambodia is hot, all the time. Scorching, burning hot. But, don't fear, it's survivable and more than that, if you do it right it actually becomes quite comfortable and dare is say enjoyable.

Why do I say enjoyable? To be honest, the heat for forces you to be relaxed. You can't 'dress up', there's no need for bags and bags of different attire. It's just not needed. It's casual and enables you to pack refreshingly light. A guy can get by with a few t-shirts, a long-sleeve shirt for the long days out temple exploring and a couple of pairs of shorts and underpants. No socks or shoes required as flip-flops are the norm.

Many women will be pleased that light comfortable boho wear is also the norm and available cheaply at the Old Market or Night Market.

Siem Reap is hottest during the months of March, April and May with temps ranging from 34-38 deg C. It's coolest during December to January with temps in the low 30's. Whilst it may not sound hot for some, when you factor in the humidity it feels like 3-4 deg hotter.

Essential Tips

Heatstroke and dehydration are real issues and you really don't want to encounter them. Here are some essential tips:

Drink plenty

You are going to sweat, day and night, and you need to replace those fluids. My own fluid intake has risen to 3-4 liters per day on an active day and I think I could be drinking more. I also try to fit a coconut in each day as they are everywhere and cheap at $1. One of the beauties of coconut water is that you can consume a lot without feeling full.

I also monitor urine color, as apparently dark yellow could be a sign of dehydration and that clear or light yellow is preferable.

Many people, including local doctors, recommend supplementing electrolytes and a popular local product is Royal-D which is available in just about every supermarket and pharmacy.

Heatstroke is very real and don't ignore it or think that somehow you are above, learn, be aware and prepare. More about heatstroke here at https://en.wikipedia.org/wiki/Heat_stroke and dehydration here at https://en.wikipedia.org/wiki/Dehydration

Clothing

You are going to have a mild sweat simply lift a cool glass of ale to your mouth, but don't worry, everybody else is too. Start walking around and the sweat increases. It's a two shirt a day kind of place. For clothing think light and airy, many manufacturers such as Under Armour, Columbia, Patagonia and even UNI-QLO make fast drying, sweat-wicking, odor-preventing shirts which are well worth looking into. I got by with standard T's as many people do. The Old Market in SR also has a lot of cheap ($8-12) Under Armour UA Tech shirts, and Nike equivalents.

Underpants are an important consideration, you might want to invest in a few pairs of Airism from UNI-QLO or another brands equivalent. Same as the shirts, they are light, breathable, quick-drying and comfortable. I didn't see anything like that on the shelves around the markets here so grab it before you come.

A scarf or Kroma as it's called locally is hugely useful. Drape it over your head and under your hat it gives a little more sun protection but mostly it helps catch any breeze and works well to keep you cool. A loose long sleeve shirt can work in the same way, catching the breeze and cooling the body. You can buy Kromas for as little as $1.50.

You'll be surprised when you take notice of the locals, most cover themselves from head to toe even in the hottest of weather. Young girls especially, wanting to hold onto their youthful skin and white complexion will cover themselves completely and maybe wear three layers plus gloves plus a hat with tinted sunshade and a scarf!

Avoiding the peak

It's hottest during 12-3pm and especially so during the months of May to April, most locals will not venture out during this time unless they have to. That's a great idea to follow. Unless you're on a one-day ticket and you're doing the fast trekking the temples, try to get most of the temple trekking done during the early hours and then head back to the hotel for a nap, swim, shower, massage or something of the like or anything out of the sun.

Sunscreen

Sunburn is no fun, and it's much healthier to use sunscreen liberally and to cover up where possible. I see many people roaming the temples in tank tops, I think that's kinda crazy, they'll be paying dearly later.

Sunscreen is easily available from any major supermarket such as Asia Market or Lucky Mall or any of the pharmacies. They stock many types 30SPF to 50SPF some with vitamin E and some from known brands such as Nivea.

Accommodation with A/C

I would generally recommend getting a room with Air Conditioning. It's not hard to find a hangout with A/C during the afternoon but come nighttime it's a blessing just to chill the room down a bit with the A/C and get a good nights sleep. If you are in a multi-level building, the lower rooms will obviously be the coolest if you have to opt for a fan only room.

Festivals and Holidays

Public Holidays

New Year's Day - January 1 - Celebrates the beginning of the Gregorian New Year

Victory Day - January 7 - Commemorates the end of the Khmer Rouge regime in 1979

Meak Bochea - February - Commemorates the ordainment of first monks to listen to the Buddha's preaching. It is celebrated in Laos, Thailand, and Cambodia where many will visit the temple and seek forgiveness for sins and recommit to Buddhist principles and values.

International Woman's Day - March 8 - Celebrating the contribution of women.

Chaul Chnam Khmer (Khmer New Year) - April 14'16 - Celebrating the Khmer New Year, it's the most important date on the calendar. While the holiday lasts for three days, the festive spirit continues for almost a month.

Visakha Puja - April or May - Commemorating the birth, enlightenment, and passing of the Buddha.

Labor Day - May 1 - Celebrates the economic and social achievements of workers.

Chat Preah Nengkal (Royal Ploughing Ceremony) - May - Cambodians have a deep connection with agriculture and this festival celebrates the beginning of the crop sewing season.

King Sihamoni's Birthday - May 13'15 - Celebrates the birthday of HM King Norodom Sihamoni (May 14, 1953).

International Children's Day - June 1 - Celebrating children and continued efforts for child rights and welfare.

Queen Mother's Birthday - June 18 - Celebrates the birthday of Queen Mother Norodom Monineath (June 18, 1936).

Constitution Day - September 24 - Celebrates the signing of the Cambodian constitution by King Sihanouk. On September 24, 1993 adopted a constitution under which the king is head of state, but the elected National Assembly has legislative power.

Pchum Ben Festival - September or October - Also known as "Ancestor's Day", locals will cook and donate food to the monks and also visit pagodas to pay respects and offer food to their ancestors and passed loved ones.

King Father's Commemoration Day - October 15 - Commemorates the memory of His Majesty Preah Bat Samdech Preah Norodom Sihanouk. Also known as 'The King-Father of Cambodia' becoming ruler of Cambodia after gaining independence from France on 9th Nov. 1953.

Paris Peace Agreement Day - October 23 - This holiday is to commemorate the Treaty of Paris on October 23, 1991, that ended war in Cambodia and created a framework for rehabilitation and reconstruction of the country.

Independence Day - November 9 - Celebrates Cambodia's independence from France in 1953.

Bon Om Touk (Water Festival) - October or November - One of the most important dates on the calendar it marks the reversal of flow of the Tonle Sap river and commemorates a festival that has been practiced since the days of the Khmer Empire when naval forces battled to be the kings champion.

Human Rights Day - December 10 - Commemorates the United Nations proclamation of the Universal Declaration of Human Rights.

Other festivals (no public holiday)

Chaul Chnam Chen (Chinese New Year Festival) - January or February - Chinese New Year is also celebrated in Cambodia due to the close cultural exchanges between the two countries and also due to the number of Chinese who have migrated here. Unique to Cambodia, Hei Neak Ta or Spirit Parade, marks the official end of the Chinese New Year celebrations.

Mid-Autumn Festival - September or October - a traditional Chinese festival, also known as Moon Festival in Cambodia.

Siem Reap Puppet Parade - February - A relatively new festival that brings the streets to life with giant puppets created by children from a multitude of local NGO projects.

Where to Stay

Siem Reap is a tourism city, it attracts a lot of visitors from Thailand, Korea, China and Japan and, especially for the Chinese, many services are tailored just for them. This is also true for western backpackers for example, places like Funky Flashpacker. Lots of locals from outside Siem Reap also come to visit the country's sacred temples and have their own style and preferences. Lots of different strokes for different folks!

The Top Hotels near the city center and Pub Street/Old Market

These hotels all receive high visitor ratings and range in price from on average $30 to 60 per night bar the more expensive Park Hyatt which averages around $240+.

Shadow Angkor Residence - https://goo.gl/UELqdn - 4 Star - French colonial-style that's very central, but quiet with river views. Also has family rooms.

Terrasse des Elephants Hotel - https://goo.gl/xuYNY2 - 4 Star - The most central hotel with a very convenient location in the heart of the central area. The hotel has a very Cambodian feel featuring colonial architecture with local traditional craft and interior design. Also has rooftop pool and spa services.

Apsara Centrepole Hotel - https://goo.gl/N5q1tC - 4 Star - Located on Sok San Road which features many small boutique restaurants it is only steps away from Pub Street and the Old Market area. The hotel has a saltwater swimming pool and spa/massage services.

Chhay Long Angkor Boutique - https://goo.gl/QWdU8s - 4 Star - a quiet location and just steps away from the Pub Street and the Old Market area. The hotel is modern and offers outdoor pool, jacuzzi, and in-house spa and wellness services. They also have a family suite.

Cheathata Suites Hotel - https://goo.gl/BteRHy - 4 Star - Another great location near to the Angkor Night Market and also offering rooftop pool and some rooms featuring a bathtub.

La Da Kiri Boutique Hotel - https://goo.gl/csD9RV - 4 Star -

Located on Sok San Road it offers an outdoor pool, free airport shuttle, rooms with bathtub, and great location.

The Tito Suite Residence - https://goo.gl/2qN8CG - 4 Star - A new hotel offering swimming pool, nice sized rooms and bathtub.

The Night Hotel - https://goo.gl/c1RncY - Just within walking distance of Pub Street and the Old Market area this hotel offers a swimming pool and free airport shuttle. It's on Sok San Road where you will find a number of smaller bars and cafe/restaurants.

Chronivada Residence - https://goo.gl/aot6QG - 5 Star - a modern and elegant hotel in a quiet but very convenient location. The hotel features fitness centre, swimming pool, and spa.

Royal Crown Hotel & Spa - https://goo.gl/Mwdj8X - 5 Star - This hotel is located across the river from the Old Market and Pub Street but just within comfortable walking distance. It is only metres away from the Riverside Night Market and Made in Cambodia Market/Kings Road where there is a cluster of cafes and restaurants including Hard Rock Cafe and Costa Coffee.

Park Hyatt Siem Reap - https://goo.gl/Hsp8Cc - 5 Star - Located on Sivatha Blvd it's only just within comfortable walking distance of the Old Market and Pub Street the hotel offers indoor and outdoor swimming pools and 3 dining options including the popular Glasshouse Deli. It also offers a 24HR gym, steam room, hot tub and spa services.

The Top Guesthouses near the city center and Pub Street/Old Market

Guesthouse prices range from $10 to 20 per night.

Cheng Lay Guesthouse - https://goo.gl/92JBzA - offers free airport shuttle, free wifi, on-site restaurant and family rooms.

Garden Village Guesthouse - https://goo.gl/4bv46m - offers a swimming pool, free wifi, and on-site restaurant.

Golden Papaya Guesthouse - https://goo.gl/Te3FZL - fan or A/C rooms available all with private bathroom.

Kandal Village Inn - https://goo.gl/gHEXSz - A/C rooms with cable TV and en suites. Free wifi and restaurant on site.

I Lodge - https://goo.gl/2mHNCF - A/C rooms and en suite bathrooms available.

Big Lyna Villa & Homestay - https://goo.gl/BPMKbo - offering more traditional Khmer style rooms and free airport shuttle. Rooms include A/C, cable TV, a fridge and private bathroom.

The Top Backpacker hostels near the city center and Pub Street/Old Market

Dormitory bed prices start at $4 and private rooms are similar to guest house prices.

Funky Flashpacker - https://goo.gl/gv3Emw - The music doesn't stop here and it's one of the most popular hostels in the city. Featuring two roof-top bars, swimming pool, ATM, mini mart, free wifi and bicycle rentals. Offers dorm style accommodation with fan and some rooms with A/C and private rooms with fan and some with A/C.

One Stop Hostel - https://goo.gl/neqX9B - Offering a rooftop bar, free wifi, and single beds in mixed dormitory rooms with air conditioning.

I Bed Hostel - https://goo.gl/3ZYmqb - Breakfast included, free airport shuttle, free wifi, and the choice of A/C or fan dorm rooms.

Onederz Hostel Siem Reap - https://goo.gl/zBuETW - Featuring both private rooms and dormitories and all rooms have A/C, roof top swimming pool, and laundry services.

Adventure Hostel Siem Reap - https://goo.gl/17Nr39 - offering free wifi, dorm rooms or private rooms all with A/C.

Hangout - https://goo.gl/kXQAyZ - a family-friendly hostel with a popular in-house restaurant. Offering dorm beds and private dorm areas.

Experience-Based and Spa Hotels

If you like to relax at the hotel, enjoy its services and amenities, and don't care to be near pub street, then this list is for you. The accommodation choices here have all been chose based on their amenities/value offer, and all have 9.5 out of 10 or higher visitor ratings!

Farm stay - https://goo.gl/uoZgrX - an insight into real Cambodian life and rural life. Free wifi is available and meals are available.

Navutu Dreams Resort & Wellness Retreat - https://goo.gl/EVQbSb - 5 Star - Offering 3 swimming pools, 2 yoga studios, a fitness centre and a restaurant.

Suorkear Boutique Hotel & Spa - https://goo.gl/sj2WW1 - 4 Star - Outdoor pool, family rooms, spa and wellness centre, steam room, hot tub, a'la carte restaurant, rooftop bar and free wifi. Some rooms have private pools. Free transport to and from the city.

UngD Angkor Suites - https://goo.gl/dbz9Fv - 4 Star - Offers spa and wellness centre, outdoor pool, hot tub, garden, free bikes, free transfers, on-site restaurant, and bar.

Belmond La Residence d'Angkor - https://goo.gl/Z6HsYz - 5 Star - Set amongst private gardens the hotel offers in-house restaurant, bar, an outdoor swimming pool, jacuzzi, fitness and spa centre equipped with a sauna.

Phum Baitang - https://goo.gl/Sf1wHL - 5 Star - offers unique luxury wooden stilt villa accommodation set amongst lush gardens and rice fields. Features include swimming pool, gym, sauna, spa and wellness centre, free airport shuttle and more.

Templation Hotel - https://goo.gl/m6T967 - 5 Star - offering outdoor pool, spa, gym, garden and villas with private pools.

Sofitel Angkor Phokeethra Golf & Spa Resort - https://goo.gl/odS1yV - 5 Star - featuring a golf course, spa centre, gym, hot tub, pool, terrace, and garden.

Renting an Apartment for Long Stays

If you're going to be staying in Siem Reap for more than a few weeks then you will probably want to negotiate something cheaper than hotel or hostel rack rates. Here's an intro to how it all plays out here in Siem Reap.

Fortunately, there are loads of places that offer short term and long term rentals, ranging from hotel-style rooms in resort style hostels to self-contained apartments, and even luxury villas.

For short-term rentals on a month by month basis, there is a lot of supply in the slow months of June, July, and September. It gets a little harder to find in the peak months as hostels and resorts would rather fill up with full rate nightly visitors. Regardless, there are still places, but they won't be at a discount.

For apartment rental, most will require the signing of a contract and require you to stay at least three months and in most cases 6 or 12 months. An amount equal to one month's rent is held as bond and one month's rent is paid in advance.

If you have a fridge, TV and use the air conditioner you can expect to pay between $50-65 each month for electricity and about $4 for water. But different landlords will charge different amounts. As a general indicator electricity is charged at 25c for 1KW and water at 75c for one cubic meter.

Most will include free wi-fi and free cable TV with 80 or so channels that include the English channels BBC News, CNBC, CNN, History Channel, Discovery, Nat Geo, Fox Movies and a few others.

Some will include free garbage collection, and free room cleaning once per week and at some places, you may pay a small fee.

Rental prices for anything within 3km of Pub Street will start at 150 per month for a basic hotel style room with A/C and bathroom but no kitchen. Your mid-range apartment that's comfortable and has it's own kitchen and maybe even washing machine will begin at 280 per month and two-bedroom apartments will begin at over 300.

There are several luxury properties which start from 500 per month and a multi-floor luxury villa with a pool maybe over 1000 per month as a general indication.

If you need something really cheap, there are 70-100 per month rooms but they are far from town and would require owning a motorbike and this may well suit some people, others not so much.

About rental contracts and landlords, this is the wild wild west, there are no laws and no one to enforce them unless you are the highest bidder. So keep good relations with your landlord if getting your bond back is important. Another note about bond money, I would recommend not giving it to an agent and rather try to hand it to the owner. Many agents are here one week and gone the next.

Where to find rental apartments?

Of course you can use real estate agents but of course, they will be taking a fee and in most cases, you can deal just directly with the owner particularly if it's a hostel/resort that is doing long-term rentals. For villas, you may need an agent where there may be language barriers.

Many properties will display 'For rent' signs. So, once you are here, hire a bike and ride around and dial away.

The next option is Facebook, there are several groups where properties are advertised regularly both by owners and by agents, they are:

https://www.facebook.com/groups/siemreap/

https://www.facebook.com/groups/siemreapforum/

Which area is the best?

I don't think any area is better than another, it really depends on your lifestyle and what you fancy. If you don't have plans on renting or owning a motorbike or bike then you should definitely choose a place that is central to the Pub Street or Night Market/Sok San Road area or at least close to a supermarket and a place that is connected by paved roads.

Recommended

Kool Apartments - https://www.facebook.com/apartmentsiemreap/ - Modern, clean serviced apartments with gym and pool. Prices from $280 per month.

Transport

Tuk Tuk (remorque)

The prime way to get around is by tuk-tuk, and they are everywhere. To go anywhere in the central area is usually 2 dollars if it's a short way you can push for a dollar. A little further and you may need to pay more.

For temple tours, you can negotiate your own rate depending on what you'd like to see. Starting rates would be 15 dollars for the small circuit and up from that.

All the drivers I have met are friendly and helpful. They are quite proactive in getting your business, they have to be because there are simply so many tuk-tuks, and some days, they may only get a couple of fares. You can negotiate the rates for daily hire or tours. BUT, not all drivers are equal, some come from the village in search of fast cash and have no or little idea of the whereabouts of the local attractions. Find an experienced driver and his/her (99.9% of the drivers are male) local knowledge will make all the difference to how much you get out of your time here.

Recommended Tuk Tuk drivers

Virak - https://www.facebook.com/tuktukvirak/

Narith - https://www.facebook.com/profile.php?id=100008369865442

Motodup

Motorbike taxis, or moto/motodup, are almost as ubiquitous as tuk-tuks. If you are traveling by yourself it's a great way to save as they are generally half price of tuk-tuks. Walk out of any bar, or cafe and there'll likely be someone plying for your business. $1 gets you almost anywhere in the city center.

Private Taxi

There are numerous private cars available for hire which can take you around the temples or to outlying attractions, or to other cities such as Poipet, Battambang or Phnom Penh. Most hotels, hostels and tour agencies can assist with finding a car and driver for any purpose. Alternatively here are some recommended options.

Siem Reap Shuttle - http://www.siemreapshuttle.com - a small fleet of modern vehicles offering private taxi services and tours.

Angkor Cab - http://angkor.cab - Sedan and Mini-Van

Blue Mobility - https://www.blue-mobility.com.kh - fully electric eco-friendly cars

Victoria Angkor - http://www.victoriaangkorhotel.com – The hotel has a pair of beautiful vintage circa 1930 Citroen's available for city tours and Angkor tours.

Bus

Siem Reap to Phnom Penh - 6.5HRS - Giant Ibis - $17

Siem Reap to Battambang - 3HRS - Mekong Express - $7

Siem Reap to Bangkok Thailand – Nattakan $28 - Giant Ibis $32

Siem Reap to Vientiane, Laos - $56.00

Siem Reap to Pakse, Laos - $30.00

For buying bus tickets online try http://camboticket.com or https://bookmebus.com

Mekong Express - https://catmekongexpress.com - Buses to and from Phnom Penh, Sihanoukville, Battambang, Poipet, Ho Chi Minh (Vietnam), Bangkok (Thailand). Modern and comfortable vehicles - Sivatha Blvd near DHL.

Giant Ibis - http://giantibis.com - Buses to and from Phnom Penh, Sihanoukville, and Bangkok. Modern buses. Office at the river end of Sivatha Blvd near the roundabout.

Nattakan Transportation - http://www.nattakan-transport.com - Siem Reap to Bangkok direct.

Capitol Tours - http://www.capitoltourscambodia.com/index.php?page_id=4 - buses to Phnom Penh, Sihanoukville, Battambang, Poipet. CNR of

Boat

You can get to Phnom Penh by boat which takes around 6 hours and costs $35. Most people would recommend the bus over this option.

You can a boat from Siem Reap to Battambang which takes around 8 to 10 hours and costs around $25. Many people highly enjoy the trip as it passes through many riverside villages and some beautiful natural scenery. Some report that it's hot, long and tiring. Up to you.

Tickets for either are available at tour agents and hotel desks.

Rent a Motorbike/scooter

A popular way to get around if you like to go your own way. It costs between $7-12 per day depending on the type of bike and discount for length of rental. Monthly rentals are generally around $100 per month. You can hire a petrol powered bike under 125cc and not required to have a license. A full tank of fuel ($3) will last several days. Many hotels and hostels rent bikes directly and there is also a cluster of bike renting shops near the Park Hyatt. To rent a bike you'll need to leave your ID (passport) as a deposit.

You can also rent electric bikes, there are charging stations throughout the Angkor park and around town. Visit Green e-bike - http://www.greene-bike.com – Street 6.

Rent a Bicycle

Bicycle rental shops are ubiquitous and you can rent a bike starting at $1 a day. Most hostels will offer bikes for rent and there are many rental places along Taphul Road or BBU Road near the roundabout. Most hostels/hotels where you stay will have bikes for rent or easily help you get one.

Siem Reap Airport and Flights

Siem Reap-Angkor International Airport (IATA: REP, ICAO: VDSR) is the busiest airport in Cambodia in terms of passenger traffic serving almost 3.5m passengers in 2016. The small airport is very relaxed and easy to navigate, so you will have no concerns getting lost here.

After departing the plane you'll have a short walk across the tarmac (have a hat and shades in your carry on) and into the terminal where you will enter customs, fill out a simple arrival card and visa application form (See the Visas section for more info). Once the form is filled out you'll stand in line and hand over your money, passport, photo and forms to the officer who will quickly check the details and then you'll move around to the waiting area and when your passport is done they'll hold it up in the air to get your attention.

Exit customs, grab your bags and head out. If you have experienced any of the large airports in the world you are going to love the simple, breezy nature of this one.

The airport is open from 6 am to 1 am. Services and facilities at the airport include free WiFi, baggage wrap services, money changers, ATM, and various food and beverage options. Starbucks is a recent addition. There are also telco stores as you exit the airport where you can buy a local sim card, see the Wifi and Sim Card section for details.

Plaza Premium Lounge, located at the International Departure Terminal, offers comfortable seating, shower facilities with amenities, VIP room, massage treatment services, recharging stations, Wi-Fi, plus meals and drinks. At the time of writing the fees were 39 USD for 2 hours and 55 USD for 5 hours.

The airport itself is located some 6 km outside Siem Reap and the most popular way to get to and from the airport is via Tuk-Tuk which you can book at the transport desk in the airport. From the airport to the city will cost around 6 USD. You can also book vans and taxis. For those with pre-booked transfers which many hotels provide, the driver will be waiting at the arrivals section with your name on a signboard.

Airlines and direct flights to/from Siem Reap

AirAsia - Kuala Lumpur, Bangkok, Phuket

Air Busan - Busan

Air China - Beijing

Air Seoul - Seoul'Incheon

Asiana Airlines - Seoul'Incheon

Bangkok Airways - Bangkok

Bassaka Air - Phnom Penh

Cambodia Angkor Air - Beijing, Chengdu, Da Nang, Guilin, Hangzhou, Guangzhou, Hanoi, Hong Kong, Ho Chi Minh City, Nanning, Phnom Penh, Seoul-Incheon, Sihanoukville, Shanghai'Pudong, Tianjin

Cambodia Bayon Airlines - Phnom Penh, Sihanoukville

Cathay Dragon - Hong Kong

Cebu Pacific - Manila

China Eastern Airlines - Chengdu, Kunming, Shanghai'Pudong

China Southern Airlines - Guangzhou

Eastar Jet - Seoul'Incheon

HK Express - Hong Kong

Jetstar Asia Airways - Singapore

Lao Airlines - Pakse

Malaysia Airlines - Kuala Lumpur

Shandong Airlines - Jinan

SilkAir - Singapore

Sky Angkor Airlines - Chengdu, Guiyang, Dalian, Hefei, Kunming, Nanchang, Nanning, Ningbo, Pusan, Sihanoukville, Seoul'Incheon, Wuhan

Spring Airlines - Shanghai

Thai Smile - Bangkok

Vietnam Airlines - Da Nang, Hanoi, Ho Chi Minh

XiamenAir - Xiamen

Keeping Safe and Health issues

Traffic Accidents

Perhaps the highest cause of injury and hospitalization in Siem Reap. It's a place where you need to pay attention and be aware of your surroundings.

This is especially so for people like you and me that perhaps come from countries where there are highly developed and enforced road rules. Similar to the rest of Asia, Siem Reap is the Wild Wild West when it comes to road rules. Vehicles, motos, and tuk-tuks use both sides of the road, turn at will, speed, cut in front and so on. Through western eyes it looks chaotic, rule breakers running wild, and a recipe for disaster. For locals it's quite different, they understand each other, theirs no road rage, and for the most part things flow in a sort of chaotic harmony, locals know when to yield, know when to push forward, and they know the flow. You don't, at least yet.

Tips for surviving the roads of Siem Reap:

Every street is not a pedestrian street. Really, you can't walk four abreast on your journey back to the hostel!

Don't stand in the middle of the road discussing your big night at the Temple Bar and how beers are cheaper than water.

When you ride a bike, wear a helmet.

When you ride a scooter, slowly slowly. I have seen so many visitors jump on scooters and do really stupid shit. Kids often walk out onto streets and running down a local isn't what you want on your holiday. You can fall off by yourself, no one will care, literally. Just don't do harm to others.

Understand, there are no rules, or right and wrong, just learn to yield and when the time is right, push forward and take your path. It's a constant process of yielding and going, yielding and going.

Respect the hierarchy. Trucks take precedent over buses, buses take precedence over cars, cars take precedence over motos and scooters, and scooters take precedence over bikes. You'll learn this quickly when riding a bike, cars and motos will zoom in front of you as if you don't even exist. Just yield.

A green light doesn't mean go. It means look, and if its safe, then go.

Mosquitoes, Dengue Fever and Malaria

Mosquitoes are going to bite you no matter what you try to do, it's Cambodia. Although, with that said, personally I have not had any real experiences to say that mosquitoes are any worse in Siem Reap than other parts of the world. I have never purchased deet, or any other type of repellent. But, I am going to be a responsible travel writer and like all the others I am going to suggest that you slather yourself in Deet, the only scientifically validated repellant, and march onwards.

Other repellent techniques include wearing light long sleeve clothing and sleep in a room with screening to keep the mosquitoes out, or use a net over the bed.

Dengue fever causes a high fever and symptoms that include a headache, joint pain, nausea, vomiting, pain behind the eyes, swollen glands and rash. On the first infection, symptoms may be mild and flu-like lasting only a few days. Serious infections, which apparently are more common when infected a second or third time, may lead to a severe form of dengue fever, called dengue hemorrhagic fever which can be life-threatening.

Dengue fever is transmitted by mosquitoes that bite during the day and it's more likely to be contracted in the urban areas.

Malaria is a life-threatening disease and fortunately as stated by IAMAT "The city of Phnom Penh is risk-free. There is low risk of malaria transmission at Angkor Wat and in the city centre of Siem Reap.". In my time here I have never heard of any cases of malaria, that said you should know that this is not the case for other parts of Cambodia where there is high risk and you need to be prepared.

Before leaving home you should discuss both of these conditions with your doctor and seek their recommendations.

Shots and Vaccines

You should discuss this with your doctor well in advance. They may recommend immunization for

Cholera: spread through consumption of contaminated water and food.

Hepatitis A: spread through consuming contaminated food and water or person to person through the fecal-oral route.

Hepatitis B: spread through infected blood and blood products, contaminated needles and medical instruments and sexual intercourse.

Japanese Encephalitis: spread through the bite of an infected mosquito.

Rabies: spread through the saliva of an infected animal, usually through a bite, scratch or lick on broken skin.

Tetanus: spread through contamination of cuts, burns, and wounds with tetanus spores.

Typhoid: spread mainly through consumption of contaminated food and drink.

Travel Warnings

Always keep abreast of the latest travel warnings and recommendations from your government.

Australia - http://smartraveller.gov.au

UK - https://www.gov.uk/foreign-travel-advice

USA - https://travel.state.gov

Canada - https://travel.gc.ca

Water

Don't drink water unless it's been boiled. Bottled water is available aplenty and costs from 50 cents per 1.5 litre bottle.

Pharmacies

UCare Pharmacy - http://u-carepharmacy.com - Hospital Road (at the end of Pub Street), Siem Reap. Location 2: In Lucky Mall on Sivatha Road. Several other locations.

Preah Vihear Pharmacy - 3 locations including one on Tep Vong St. Good range and good service.

Hospitals and Clinics

Royal Angkor Hospital - http://www.royalangkorhospital.com - best local medical facility - Route 6 Airport Rd, Siem Reap: (063) 761 888

British Khmer Clinic - http://www.britishkhmerclinic.com - British doctor, Dr Ian Ferguson - House A73 Charles De Gaulle, Siem Reap

Lysreyvyna Medical Group - http://www.lysreyvynaclinic.com - 24-hour services - #113 National Route 6, Siem Reap; (063) 965 088

Doctors Rithy Kong and Sok Leng: Consultations $5 - no appointment necessary. Behind Akira Electrical, #11, National Route 6, Siem Reap; (012) 832 152

Police

Tourist Police - office opposite the ticket booths for the Angkor Archaeological Park - PH (012) 402 424.

Language Basics

You needn't worry too much about learning to speak Khmer to get by on your holiday as English is widely spoken. Speaking a little Khmer, or at least trying, will get rounds of applause and smiles from locals, and it's a lot of fun too and learning a few words from a local speaker is another part of Khmer culture that you carry with you always.

Here are some basic phrases in Khmer:

Common Phrases

Hello - Sours'dey (informal)

Good morning - Arun sours'dey

How are you? - Sok-sabai tay?

Fine thanks - Sok-sabai

Goodbye - Lee Hai

My name is... - Kgnom tchmuu....

What is your name? - Neak tchmuu ay?

Good luck! - Samnang la'aw

Thank you - Akun

Sorry - Sohm-toe

Never mind - Ot-a-tay

Do you understand? - Jol-ay?

How much does this cost? - Tlay ponmaan?

Very expensive - Tlay na

The bill please - Sohm gket loy

Turn left - Baat chwein

Turn right - Baat sadaam

Straight ahead - Muk tiet

Stop here - Chup tii nii

Slow down - Yut-yut

Yes - Chaa (female) Bah (male)

No - Otay

I agree - Nung ay

Do you have...? - Miean-ay...?

Do not have/there is no - Ot mien

Eat (general) - Gnaam bai

Drink - Gnaam phhak

Places

Hotel - Phateya-samnaq

House - Phateya

Post office - Poh

Market - Psaa

Shop - Haang

Days of the week

Monday - Tnay jahn

Tuesday - Tnay angkia

Wednesday - Tnay phut

Thursday - Tnay bprahoah

Friday - Tnay sok

Saturday - Tnay sao

Sunday - Tnay atuut

Numbers

1 Muy

2 Pii

3 Bey

4 Boun

5 Pram

6 Pram-muy

7 Pram-pii

8 Pram-bey

9 Pram-boun

10 Dop

20 Maphey

30 Samsup

40 Saesup

50 Haasup

60 Hoksup

70 Chetsup

80 Paetsup

90 Kawsup

100 Ma roi

1,000 Ma poun

10,000 Ma moern

Want to learn how to speak proficiently? You can learn more from Youtube where there a handful of free user-submitted videos on learning Khmer or do a course here in Siem Reap, contact https://www.facebook.com/learnkhmerREP/ or https://www.facebook.com/speaklikekhmer/

Seasons and Weather

Siem Reap is hot, and sweaty, but not impossibly so. Dress smart and plan smart and you'll have no trouble here. Take a read of the section on Beating the Heat.

November-February: The most comfortable weather period of the year, and the most popular months with visitors. There are only small chances of rain and the temperatures cool off night to comfortable mid 20's and the day's peak in the low 30's.

March-May: In short, hot and dry. There is little rain and the temps climb up into the mid to high 30's with humidity to boot. It's the hottest part of the year and there is little escape from it. Late March is significant due to the equinox when the sun rises directly over the temple spires of Angkor Wat, the only other time this happens is in late September.

June-August: It still hot but almost predictable afternoon showers provide a comforting respite. The rain showers pass quickly and shouldn't deter you from going about your day. Temps hit highs of mid 30's but start to cool off through June/August.

September-Early November: It's still hot, but compared to the other parts of the year it's quite cool, the rains can be intense but never overly disrupting. The countryside is lush and green and the ponds at the temple fill to a peak. The river through town looks beautiful as it fills and clears away the algae and rubbish it collects throughout the rest of the year. September is also special due to the equinox when the sun will rise directly above the temple spires of Angkor Wat which happens in late September.

Siem Reap and Angkor History

In this section I'll try to give an overly brief intro in the history of the Khmer Empire and modern Cambodia. Think of it as a primer rather than a definitive outline, for deeper insight there are a couple of suggested books at the end.

The beginning of the Khmer civilization dates back to around 1000 BC and it's early days began with forging trade with what we now know as India and China, along with soaking up culture and religious beliefs from both. While early history is sketchy and almost nonexistent, it's also speculated that there were linkages to Java (Indonesia) and deep connections with Tamil. Beyond speculation, most of the written knowledge of early Khmer history comes from a Chinese diplomat Zhou Daguan who began a year-long visit to Angkor beginning in 1296.

When Zhou Daguan visited at that time the Khmer Empire was well and truly in the midst of its golden age. From its capital Angkor, the Khmer Empire at times held sway over territory that includes present-day Cambodia, Laos, Thailand, and southern Vietnam. The empires beginning owes itself to King Jayavarman II who, after uniting areas through conquest, declared himself the Universal Monarch, or God King, and in 802 the Khmer Kingdom was born.

Jayavarman II ruled from 802-835, claimed as the founder of the Khmer Kingdom.

Jaravarman III ruled from 835-877 and not much is known about his time.

Indravarman I ruled from 877-889 and led major construction programs with the notable remaining structure being Preah Ko.

In 889, Yasovarman ascended to the throne where he stayed until 900. His legacy that stands today is Phnom Bakheng.

It was a revolving door leading to throne with five leaders coming and going until Rajendravarman II (reigned 944 - 968) took the helm and began building again, which included Pre Rup, East Mebon, and several Buddhist temples and monasteries.

Jayavarman V, reigned from 968 to c. 1001. During his tenor one of the most beautiful temples that we see today, Banteay Srei, was built. Ta Keo, is another of his creations that remains today.

Suryavarman I ruled from 1002 to 1049 and is credited with beginning construction of the West Baray.

It was a revolving door that led to the throne again, five kings come and went until Suryavarman II (reigned 1113 - after 1145) got in the hot seat. And a hot seat it was, he didn't rest, and has left us with the amazing and mesmerising Angkor Wat. Not only that, he also expanded the empire to include what is now central Thailand, the northern part of the Malaysian Penninsula, and southern Vietnam.

Three kings came and went following the death of Suryavarman, and after leading and winning a brief war with invading Cham forces (Southern Vietnamese), Jayavarman VII (reigned from 1181-1219) became king and got busy building what we can still see today, Angkor Thom, Bayon Temple, Ta Prohm and Preah Khan. It was a golden time for the Khmer empire, laying claim to being the largest city in the world and the most advanced civilisation behind the Chinese. This was also the time that the empire converted from Hinduism to Buddhism.

Following the death of Jayavarman VII in 1219, Indravarman II took the helm and was followed by Jayavarman VIII who returned the empire to Hinduism. Jayavarman VIII was followed by another revolving door of kings going in and out during which time the empire entered a slow decline and even fell to invasion from Thai forces.

It wasn't until King Barom Reachea I (reigned 1566 – 1576) that the Thai forces were repelled. But, the empire was still in decline and would become a battleground for control by Thai and opposing Viet forces seeking hegemony.

Thailand had taken over Battambang and Siem Reap including Angkor and the Vietnamese had the rest. The Thai and Viet forces fought for control until an agreement was reached for shared control. The Khmer continued to fight for independence and it was under King Duang that a relationship with the French began in an effort to secure Cambodia from Thai and Viet suzerainty.

King Duang was succeeded by his son, Norodom, yet he was never crowned due to a dispute between the Vietnamese and Thais until 1863 when the French, already controlling parts of Vietnam and wishing to keep the British out of the Mekong, entered the fray.

By 1866 the French had negotiated for Norodom to be crowned King and for Cambodia to be proclaimed a French protectorate. After a rebellion and death of the king, in 1897 the French had assumed executive authority over Cambodia. Norodoms brother, Sisowath (ruled 1904 to 1927) was proclaimed king and worked with the French during a time that saw Siem Reap and Battambang returned to Cambodian rule along with the paving of roads and other infrastructure.

During World War II the Japanese overthrew French occupation and Cambodia oddly had gained independence, yet it was to be short-lived, at the end of the WWII the French returned and took control over Cambodia, declaring it 'autonomous state within the French Union'. Political parties were created along with a constitution.

Without digging too deep into a historical rabbit hole, in 1946 the first of the Indochina Wars had begun between France and Vietnam, ending in 1954 with an agreement at a Geneva Conference to end the war and divide Vietnam into a north and south. At that same conference, Cambodia won its independence with Prince Norodom Sihanouk's government being recognized as the sole legitimate authority within Cambodia.

This wasn't going to be the dream ride everyone expected, Asian democracies never are, there were tales of authoritarianism, infighting, dodgy elections and amongst all that, a school teacher, Saloth Sar, who would flee to Vietnam and create what would later be known as the Khmer Rouge.

In 1970, Cambodia's National Assembly voted to remove Prince Sihanouk from office. Sihanouk went to Beijing for help and an alliance was formed with Beijing, North Vietnam and Solath Sar who was now leading Cambodian Communist forces.

The new government in Cambodia was determined to fight off these communist forces but was largely unsuccessful, even with large assistance from the US. The communists eventually gained control of Cambodia. Much like Mao Zedong's China, private enterprise was abolished, and communist philosophies were ruling over the land. Prince Sihanouk resigned, merely a figurehead by that stage apparently, following which the country was declared Democratic Kampuchea and Pol Pot became prime minister. Who was Pol Pot? Saloth Sar.

Conservative estimates are that between April 1975 and early 1979, when the regime was overthrown, at least 1.5 million Cambodians, about 20 percent of the total population, died from overwork, starvation, disease, or execution.

Through intervention by Vietnamese forces, Pol Pot was forced onto the sidelines and Vietnam installed its own regime. In the confusion and disorder of such change people fled by the thousands to Thailand and other countries. Vietnam was no hero here, and opposition forces rallied on the borders, many financed by other countries.

Cutting this long, dark story short, and it's a story that deserves to be read in full, combined efforts of the US through sanctions and Russia's withdrawal of aid saw the Vietnamese withdraw. The

United Nations acted as a peacekeeper in the region and managed a transitional authority until elections were held, and the United National Front, by a clear majority, were elected to govern.

But wait, things are never that easy are they, the Cambodian People's Party (CPP) and the former prime minister, Hun Sen, refused to accept the results of the election. A deal was made for the United National Front to create a coalition government with the Cambodian People's Party led by Hun Sen.

In 1998, there was a coup, a brutal one, and Hun Sen took absolute authority. Wait, there are more twists and turns. The leader of the UNF, Prince Ranariddh, was forced into exile, later exonerated, and in the following election, due to the CCP not being able to form a majority, saw him and his party being invited to form a coalition again.

Oh my, the poor suffering people of this land! The next time you want to get in a fluff about the way your president waved or shook someone's hand, I am sure you'll think twice!

On a brighter note, the World Bank reports that in 2014, the poverty rate was 13.5% compared to 47.8% in 2007, and that Cambodia has sustained an average growth rate of 7.6% in 1994-2015, ranking sixth in the world. Lets hope for continued and growing prosperity.

Let's backtrack a little bit and get back to the topic of Angkor. Whilst Angkor was never 'lost', the first western interactions with abandoned city was apparently a Portuguese Capuchin friar named Antonio da Magdalena in 1586, followed by Gabriel Quiroga de San Antonio, followed by a Japanese pilgrim sometime in the early 17th century, a French missionary, Charles-Emile Bouillevaux, visited in 1850 who was later followed by a French naturalist that would capture the excitement and attention of the world with his detailed descriptions and drawings, Henri Mouhot in 1860.

In 1901 the Ecole Francaise D'Extreme-Orient (EFEO) began their long relationship with Angkor by funding an expedition into Siam to the Bayon. The EFEO cleared and restored the whole site, and rediscovered many of the surrounding temples. In the same year, the first tourists arrived in Angkor, 200 of them in three months. Up until this point, what the world now knows as 'Siem Reap city' was little more than a small rural village near the Tonle Sap Lake.

Siem Reap in the past 15 years has grown from a village into a city that is home to over 200,000 people and sees over 2 million people annually coming to visit its ancient temples. Today Siem Reap is home to world-class resorts and global brand luxury hotels, world-class golf course, high-end restaurants and luxury spas, yet, it still holds its wonderous and characterful dusty village charm.

It's a city that's growing fast with a new airport and rail line set to begin development in 2018, a new shopping complex set to open in 2018 along with several new markets and attractions. If you are a fan of the laid back village experience, capture it while you can as this city is on a growth trajectory fueled by Chinese investment.

Further Reading:

Pol Pot: Anatomy of a Nightmare by Philip Short. ISBN-10: 0805080066

How did an idealistic dream of justice and prosperity mutate into one of the humanity's worst nightmares? To answer these questions, Short traveled through Cambodia, interviewing former Khmer Rouge leaders and sifting through previously closed archives around the world.

A History of Cambodia by David Chandler ISBN-10: 1578566967

Praised by the Journal of Asian Studies as an 'original contribution, superior to any other existing work,' this acclaimed text has now been completely revised and updated to include material examining the early history of Cambodia, whose famous Angkorian ruins now attract more than one million tourists each year, the death of Pol Pot, and the revolution and final collapse of the Khmer Rouge.

Misc. & Useful Contacts

Sending Mail and Packages

DHL - 15A Sivatha Blvd. PH: +855 63 964 949

Post Office - mail and parcels via EMS. Pokambor Ave (between street 3 and Oum Khun St)

Airport

Siem Reap International Airport - 063 962 400

Hospitals and Clinics

Royal Angkor Hospital - http://www.royalangkorhospital.com - Route 6 Airport Rd, Siem Reap - 063 761 888

British Khmer Clinic - http://www.britishkhmerclinic.com - British doctor, Dr. Ian Ferguson - House A73 Charles De Gaulle, Siem Reap

Lysreyvyna Medical Group - http://www.lysreyvynaclinic.com - 24-hour services - #113 National Route 6, Siem Reap - 063 965 088

Ambulance

Royal Angkor International Hospital - 063 761 888

Neak Tep Clinic Ambulance Service - 017 928 655 or 015 883 899

Police and Fire and Gov

Tourist Police - office opposite the ticket booths for the Angkor Archaeological Park - 012 402 424.

110

Fire Department - 012 784 464

Ministry of Tourism: 023 211 593

Ministry of Foreign Affairs and International Cooperation: 023 214 441

Department of Immigration: 023 890 380 / 012 434 849 / 012 856 233

21779012R00069

Printed in Great Britain
by Amazon